MW00814324

Nietzsche's Rhetoric

Francesca Cauchi

Nietzsche's Rhetoric

Four Case Studies

Francesca Cauchi 🆔
Department of Foreign Languages & Literature
National Sun Yat-sen University
Kaohsiung City, Taiwan

ISBN 978-3-031-42963-7   ISBN 978-3-031-42964-4   (eBook)
https://doi.org/10.1007/978-3-031-42964-4

Cover pattern © Melisa Hasan

This Palgrave Macmillan imprint is published by the registered company Springer Nature Switzerland AG.
The registered company address is: Gewerbestrasse 11, 6330 Cham, Switzerland

Paper in this product is recyclable.

ACKNOWLEDGMENTS

I would first like to thank Teun De Rycker for meticulously proofreading the final draft of this book and flagging the more unwieldy sentences. I am also indebted to Trevor Hope for his comments and suggestions on earlier drafts of the Introduction and Appendix. Thanks are also due to the National Science and Technology Council of Taiwan for a generous research grant.

CONTENTS

Abbreviations

WS   *The Wanderer and His Shadow* (Part Two of *Human All Too Human*, vol. 2)
Z   *Thus Spoke Zarathustra: A Book for Everyone and No-One*
ZP   'Zarathustra's Prologue'
Z1–4   *Zarathustra*: Parts 1 to 4

Citations & Translations

Bracketed citations to Nietzsche's works follow the standard English abbreviations listed above, followed by aphorism number (e.g. GS 125, BGE 45), or by abbreviated chapter title followed by numbered subsection (e.g. TI 'Socrates' 10 = *Twilight of the Idols*, 'The Problem of Socrates', section 10). After the English reference, volume and page number of the German source text is given (e.g. D 215, KSA 3:192 = *Daybreak*, aphorism 215; *Kritische Studienausgabe*, vol. 3, p. 192). All Nietzsche quotations in this book have been taken from the translated editions cited in the list of references appended to each chapter and occasionally modified for the sake of clarity or idiomatic style. Except where indicated, all italicized words in these translations are Nietzsche's emphases, not mine.

CHAPTER 1

Introduction

Abstract The book's core contention is that Nietzsche's rhetoric circumscribes rather than expands the reader's interpretive horizon. Contrary to the widespread view that Nietzsche's aphoristic style is light, playful, affirmative, and 'perspectival,' this chapter advances the following counterarguments. First, that many of Nietzsche's aphorisms are dogmatic, rebarbative, and heavy-handed. Second, that one of Nietzsche's key rhetorical strategies is to deploy successive aphorisms as a means of amassing 'evidence' in anticipatory support of a particular claim, thereby evincing a position firmly held and advocated for rather than expressing merely personal taste and proclivities. And third, that Nietzsche's quasi-discursive strategy has been largely overlooked due to an overemphasis on what many commentators hold to be an intrinsic connection between Nietzsche's written style and his theory of language. By shedding light on Nietzsche's rhetorical practice, the book's four case studies seek to assess the extent to which his rhetoric militates against the philosophical claims being advanced; masks internal contradictions; evinces a propensity to essentialize types; and conceals deep-seated prejudices in Nietzsche's affective-evaluative formations.

Keywords Nietzsche • Style • Aphorism • Dogmatism • Types • Prejudice • Self-contradiction

F. Cauchi, *Nietzsche's Rhetoric*,
https://doi.org/10.1007/978-3-031-42964-4_1

1

In his lecture notes on classical rhetoric, written between 1872 and 1874 during his tenure at the University of Basel, Nietzsche quotes Kant and Schopenhauer's very different characterizations of ancient rhetoric. For Kant (1961, 84), "Rhetoric is the art of transacting a serious business of the understanding as if it were a free play of the imagination." For Schopenhauer (1966, 118), on the other hand,

> Eloquence is the faculty of stirring up in others our view of a thing, or our opinion regarding it, of kindling in them our feeling about it, and thus of putting them in sympathy with us; and all this by our conducting the stream of our ideas into their heads by means of words, with such force that this stream diverts that of their own thoughts from the course already taken, and carries this away with it along its own course. The more the course of their ideas differed previously from ours, the greater will be this masterly achievement.

Nietzsche associates the first with the Greeks and the second with the Romans, noting "the commanding dominance of the individual personality" in Roman oratory (Gilman et al. 1989, 3–5). It is precisely the commanding dominance and persuasive force of Nietzsche's rhetoric, carefully calibrated to carry the reader away with it like a stream in full spate, that I shall be examining in the following four texts: 'On Truth and Lies in a Nonmoral Sense' (hereafter 'Truth and Lies'), *Daybreak*, *Beyond Good and Evil* (hereafter 'BGE'), and *Twilight of the Idols* (hereafter '*Twilight*').

The art of persuasion is a craft, and within that craft the words 'art' and 'craft' lend themselves to the same wordplay, i.e., artful, clever, skillful, artifice, stratagem, ruse, ingenious, and so forth. Indeed, as Nietzsche himself informs us in *Daybreak*, "Whenever a person reveals something, one can ask: What is it supposed to conceal? From what is it supposed to divert the eyes? What prejudice is it supposed to arouse? And additionally: How far does the subtlety of this dissimulation go? And in what way has it failed?" (D 523, KSA 3:301). It is precisely these questions which my four case studies set out to answer.

A good place to begin is Nietzsche's disarming and disingenuous "assumption" towards the end of BGE, a substantial work of almost three hundred aphorisms, "that people now know from the outset the extent to which these are only—*my* truths" (BGE 231, KSA 5:170)—and this in a work which tends to proclaim its truths with the subtlety of a sledgehammer. The phrase "these are only—*my* truths" is often taken by commentators as an expression of Nietzsche's so-called 'perspectivism,' the idea that in the absence of any definitive truths there can only be different perspectives. But as Nietzsche points out (another late admission), the personal truths expressed in aphorisms 231-239 are not truths at all, but merely entrenched prejudices. BGE 231 opens with the observation that while learning is indubitably transformational, there is deep within us "a brick wall of spiritual *fatum*, of predetermined decisions and answers to selected, predetermined questions," that is incapable of learning. An instance of this, Nietzsche continues, is the subject of men and women, upon which "a thinker cannot change his views but only reinforce them." Having thus informed the reader that there are certain subjects (e.g., the two sexes) upon which even a thinker is not really thinking but merely expressing deep-seated feelings/prejudices, Nietzsche warns us that the truths upon which he is about to pronounce (aphorisms numbered 232 to 239) pertain specifically to the aforesaid subject, namely "the 'woman *an sich.*'" Note the scare quotes here, flagging the fatuousness of the notion of an '*an sich*' (the essence of a thing), which, as Nietzsche *learnt* from Kant's epistemology, is not something to which human beings can ever have access. The inference to be drawn, then, from Nietzsche's "assumption" that the reader has known "from the outset the extent to which these are only—*my* truths" is that "these" particular truths, which are emphatically Nietzsche's truths, spring from the kind of sentiments and prejudices that are ultimately "*unteachable*" [*Unbelehrbar*]. And the reason they are unteachable is their rootedness in "the very great stupidity" that lies deep within us all (BGE 231, KSA 5:170). Clearly, the reader could not have known this "from the outset," nor have been able to distinguish one category of Nietzsche's truths from another, having not had the niceties of such a distinction explained to them at the outset.

Another example of Nietzsche playing fast and loose with the reader is his recommendation late in *Daybreak*—towards dusk, as it were—that the reader "dip into" the book (D 454, KSA 3:274). Like Nietzsche's untimely reminder of the very great stupidity within us all, his "dipping" advice comes late in the work, very late in fact, and again serves to orient the reader towards the ostensibly 'perspectival' (i.e., "*my* truths," not *the* truth) nature of Nietzsche's aphorisms.[1] It is a piece of advice, however,

---

[1] Nietzsche uses the same strategy, i.e., an eleventh hour 'revelation' to the reader, in his *Genealogy* (see the final paragraph of the 'Stacking the Deck' section in Chap. 3 of this monograph).

that obscures what in many cases is a cumulative mode of argumentation (elaborated in the next paragraph), which carries the reader along with it and masterfully diverts the stream of their own thought into that of Nietzsche's. Subtle arts such as these, together with the more conventional forms of rhetorical hoodwinking such as serial assumptions and logical fallacies, will be excavated and elucidated in the following chapters. By shedding light on Nietzsche's rhetorical practice, my critical objective is to assess the extent to which his rhetoric militates against the philosophical claims being advanced; masks internal contradictions;[2] evinces a propensity to essentialize types; and conceals deep-seated prejudices in Nietzsche's affective-evaluative formations.

As mentioned above, one of Nietzsche's key rhetorical strategies is to deploy successive aphorisms as a means of amassing 'evidence' in anticipatory support of a particular claim, thereby evincing a position firmly held and advocated for rather than merely expressing taste or personal opinion. An outstanding example of this is the first nine aphorisms of *Daybreak*, which severally and incrementally build an argument for the proposition—not announced until the ninth aphorism—that morality is nothing more than obedience to custom. The building blocks of this argument (D 1–8, KSA 3:19–21) are as follows:

D 1: What time and custom has rendered eminently rational is found to originate in the non-rational.

D 2: What the learned men of all ages have pronounced as good and evil is now known to be "a prejudice of the learned."

D 3: The "*ethical significance*" attributed to all things will one day be seen to be as fanciful as the ancients' attribution of a sex to all things, e.g., the masculine sun and the feminine moon.

D 4: We need to rid the world of much of its "*false* grandeur"—an implicit corollary of imbuing things with ethical significance.

D 5: We no longer need to live in fear of wild animals, barbarians, and gods.

---

[2] Against the view that the contradictions in Nietzsche's texts are a function of his 'perspectivism,' Staten (1990, 6) points to "the *tonality* in which Nietzsche speaks his perspectives—on women and Germans, for instance. Or the privilege he gives to one perspective while suppressing another—the poisonous effects of Christianity as opposed to its curative effects, for instance." This tonality will be addressed at length in Chap. 5 of my book, where I discuss the marked shift in tone from BGE to *Twilight*.

D 6: Whereas the conjurer (Nietzsche's implicit epithet for religion) leads us to believe in a simple causality (i.e., that God is the cause of all things), science "compels" us to abandon such beliefs.
D 7: Science teaches us to distinguish between the real and the imaginary—an implicit corollary of the beliefs mentioned in D 6.
D 8: We no longer believe in the transfigurations imagined by those who suffer helplessly, dream confusedly, and are entranced by the supernatural—an example of D 7.
QED: Morality is nothing more than obedience to custom—a pithy restatement of D 1.

This quasi-discursive strategy is one that has been largely overlooked by Nietzsche commentators. And the principal reason for this oversight, I believe, is an overemphasis on what many commentators hold to be an intrinsic connection between Nietzsche's written style and his philosophical commitments (see Appendix),[3] and the extent to which the latter is informed by his theory of language.

What we know of Nietzsche's theory of language is derived from his 1873 essay 'Truth and Lies' and his contemporaneous lecture notes for a course on rhetoric that he gave at the University of Basel in the winter semester of 1872–1873. As many commentators have pointed out, these lecture notes draw on Richard Volkmann's (1872) *Die Rhetorik der Griechen und Römer in systematischer Übersicht*, Gustav Gerber's (1872) *Die Sprache als Kunst*, and the works of Friedrich Blass (1865) on Attic oratory. Nevertheless, what is significant about these notes, argues de Man (1979, 104–105), is that "Nietzsche moves the study of rhetoric away from techniques of eloquence and persuasion by making these dependent on a previous theory of figures of speech or tropes," and that within the terms of the latter theory, "tropes are not understood aesthetically, as ornament, nor are they understood semantically as a figurative meaning that derives from literal, proper denomination. Rather, the reverse is the

---

[3] For a penetrating analysis of the different approaches taken to the question of Nietzsche's style as indicative of and inseparable from his philosophical views, see the opening chapter ('The "Problem of Style" in Nietzsche's Philosophy/The "Problem of Philosophy" in Nietzsche's Style') of Magnus et al. (1993).

case. The trope is not a derived, marginal, or aberrant form of language but the linguistic paradigm par excellence."[4]

According to Nietzsche's theory of language, elucidated in 'Truth and Lies,' language does not accurately reflect the objects it names but rather describes an ineluctably human construct. A word is merely the penultimate metaphor in a series of "artistic transference[s]" from one sphere to an entirely different sphere: successive transpositions from a nerve stimulus (sensation), to a visual metaphor (perception), to a sound metaphor (word), to a conceptual metaphor (abstraction). Accordingly, therefore, if language is irreducibly metaphorical, "metaphors which in no way correspond to the original entities" (TL 82-85, KSA 1:879–883),[5] then philosophy and its complex systems of concepts are not repositories of truth but of human perception. Viewed through the optics of this theory, Nietzsche's non-discursive style—so argue the advocates for a necessary connection between Nietzsche's style and his philosophical commitments—purposively makes explicit what in the Western philosophical tradition is concealed beneath purportedly objective accounts of reality.

The two features of Nietzsche's written style that the aforesaid advocates view as an instantiation of his thought are his prevalent use of metaphor and his predilection for the aphorism. Influential interpretations of the former are reviewed in the Appendix, but given the wealth of critical

---

[4] Regarding Nietzsche's recourse to Gerber while preparing for his lecture course on classical rhetoric, Babich (2006, 26) writes that in his 1873 essay, "Nietzsche does not merely advert to the artistic potential of Gerber's *Language as Art* as much as he seeks to push the question of truth and lie in language, importantly enough, taking the same question of language, truth, and knowledge in the tradition of language philosophy derived in turn from Wilhelm von Humboldt." For a clear and detailed exposition of Nietzsche's theory of language and consequent move away from the representational model of language—the model upon which the philosophical tradition constructs its conceptual systems and lays claim to epistemological truths—towards a rhetorical model of language, see the chapter entitled 'Language, Metaphor, Rhetoric' in Schrift (1990, 123–143). Schrift incisively demonstrates the extent to which Nietzsche's later work is grounded in his earlier insights into the tropological nature of language and, by extension, the illusory nature of both the correspondence theory of truth and the referential theory of meaning.

[5] Cf. the following passage from Nietzsche's lecture notes on ancient rhetoric, "Man, who forms language, does not perceive things or events, but *impulses*; he does not communicate sensations, but merely copies of sensations. The sensation, evoked through a nerve impulse, does not take in the thing itself: this sensation is presented externally through an image. ... It is not the things that pass over into consciousness, but the manner in which we stand toward them ... The full essence of things will never be grasped" (Rh. 21–23).

discourse on the significance of Nietzsche's aphoristic style,[6] a few preliminary observations will suffice. The first thing to bear in mind is that
Nietzsche's so-called aphorisms are sequentially numbered segments of
variable length, ranging from a few words to a sustained argument of several pages. Thus, what we normally understand by the word 'aphorism,'
i.e., a tersely worded saying or *bon mot*, only applies to Nietzsche's maxims
and epigrams. These can be found either sprinkled among the aforesaid
numbered segments or grouped under the rubric 'maxims' (see the title to
Part 1 of Volume II of *Human, All Too Human*—hereafter '*Human*'), and
'epigrams' (see the title to Part 4 of BGE and to the opening chapter of
Twilight). The second thing to note is that the idiosyncratic and highly
emotive style of Nietzsche's aphorisms can be justly viewed as a manifestation of what Nietzsche asserts to be the "unwitting [*unvermerkt*] memoir"
of every great philosophy—a memoir, that is to say, in which the affective
economy and resultant "moral (or immoral) intentions" of its author is
inscribed (BGE 6, KSA 5:19–20). Thirdly, many of Nietzsche's 'aphorisms' bear the appearance of a "thought experiment" (Kaufmann 1974,
85) in the spirit of his frequent wordplay on '*Versuch*,' meaning an attempt,
experiment, and temptation (see, for example, BGE 42, KSA 5:59[7]).
Implicit in these thought experiments is Nietzsche's well-known distrust of
all philosophical systems—"The will to a system is a lack of integrity" (TI
'Maxims and Arrows' 26, KSA 6:63)—and his concomitant objection to
the dogmatism he associates with such systems. Lastly, a number of interpreters link Nietzsche's professed anti-dogmatic stance to what they perceive to be the ludic quality of his aphoristic style. To quote Dannhauser
(1974, 197–198) on the subject, "[the Nietzsche aphorism] counters the
clumsiness and heaviness of systematic, dogmatic philosophy with lightness
and playfulness," a view which echoes Kofman's (1993, 115) assertion that
"[i]n its brevity and density, the aphorism is an invitation to dance: it is the
actual writing of the will to power, affirmative, light, and innocent."

Pace Dannhauser and Kofman, the four case studies in this volume
identify and critique what I consider to be the dogmatic, rebarbative,
heavy-handed, and far from innocent quality of many of Nietzsche's

---

[6] For a useful overview of how Nietzsche's aphoristic style has been interpreted by prominent scholars, see Nehamas (1985, 14–18).

[7] BGE 42: "A new breed of philosophers is approaching ... philosophers of the future
[who] might have the right (and perhaps also the wrong) to be called *attempters* [*Versucher*].
Ultimately, this name itself is only an attempt [*Versuch*], and, if you will, a temptation
[*Versuchung*]."

aphorisms. Now browbeating, now surreptitious, Nietzsche's rhetoric, I contend, activates a very different kind of text-reader dynamic to those elaborated by previous commentators. Dannhauser (1974, 201), for example, claims that the "deeply personal" nature of Nietzsche's aphorisms is "meant to provoke the reader to become a true self." Strong (2013, 522), on the other hand, points to the "therapeutic aim" of Nietzsche's aphoristic writing whereby the hiatus between "what the reader wants and what the text makes available and requires of the reader" generates a critical and self-critical relation between text and reader. For Kofman (1993, 114–116), the aphoristic form is fundamentally elitist, aimed at confounding and distancing the *profanum vulgus* while at the same time engaging those readers adequately "equipped with a rigorous philological art." This philological art, maintains Kofman, produces "[a] new reading/writing [which] destroys the traditional categories of the book as a closed totality containing a definitive meaning, the author's … The aphorism, by its discontinuous character, disseminates meaning and appeals to the pluralism of interpretations and their renewal."[8] Concurring with Kofman, Allison (2001, 76) argues that the aphorism is "open-ended" in its signification: It "demands" that the inquisitive reader, who becomes "immediately involved, enamored, intertwined with the aphorism," gives it meaning "by *interpreting* it, by inserting it into ever-new contexts, by directing its words to ever-new occasions, associations, events."

To reiterate, these interpretations of the text-reader dynamic in Nietzsche's works are substantially different from the one I am advancing in this book, which is not to say that the former are misconceived. On the contrary, a great deal of Nietzsche's rhetoric does indeed invite the reader to self-reflect as the necessary first step in any prospective self-transformation or self-overcoming. However, this is far from being Nietzsche's default position. As I shall demonstrate in the following case studies, many of his rhetorical strategies evince either a didactic force that overpowers our critical faculties or a rhetorical mastery that entices and entraps. Thus, while I agree with Allison that Nietzsche's aphoristic style immediately draws the "enamored" reader in, it does so not only to invite new interpretations and applications, but also to lure the reader into Nietzsche's head and

---

[8] Cf. Lambek (2020, 58–59), "Nietzsche's rhetoric is oriented toward the production of what I call 'receptive effects,' which, ideally, facilitate new, reflexive and interpretive value-creators."

heart, including that "brick wall of spiritual *fatum*, of predetermined decisions and answers to selected, predetermined questions." Once ensnared, we find ourselves uncritically acquiescing in his commendations and condemnations. Babich (2006, 19–23) likewise comments on the "seductiveness" of Nietzsche's style and insightfully draws our attention to a passage in which Nietzsche admires the stylistic expediency of the New Testament:

> [A] perspicacious man can learn from it all the expedients by which a book can be made into a universal book, a friend of everyone, and especially that master expedient of representing everything as having already been discovered, with nothing still on the way and as yet uncertain. All influential books try to leave behind this kind of impression: the impression that the widest spiritual and psychical horizon has here been circumscribed and that every star visible now or in the future will have to revolve around what shines here. (AOM 98, KSA 2:417)

In the following four chapters, summarized below, I shall endeavor to show how in many instances Nietzsche's rhetoric circumscribes rather than expands the reader's interpretive horizon.

Chapter 2 offers Nietzsche's early, unpublished essay 'On Truth and Lies in a Nonmoral Sense' as a template of his subsequent rhetorical style. A close examination of the text's use of similes, epithets, repetition, wordplay, assonance, and hyperbole will disclose, on the one hand, the rhetorical strategies by means of which Nietzsche polemically transposes the Kantian transcendental aesthetic into a moral harangue on truth and lies, arrogance and ignorance, and, on the other hand, how this heightened transposition mirrors the formation of language as expounded by Nietzsche in the essay. As noted above, if language is merely the end product of a series of metaphorical transpositions from sensation to image to sound, it necessarily lacks the authority to deliver logical, philosophical, or scientific truths. Such 'truths,' therefore, are false, but which Nietzsche rhetorically and moralistically magnifies into 'lies' begotten by human pride, arrogance, and deception. As the chapter points out, Nietzsche's use of such morally freighted terms in his re-staging of Kant's epistemological Copernican revolution incongruously belies the 'nonmoral sense' of truth and lies adverted to in the essay's title, thereby furnishing an early example of the kind of titular-textual misalignment also found in *Twilight* (see Chap. 5).

Chapter 3 presents Nietzsche's *Daybreak* account of the genealogy of morals—an important precursor to the later and better known *On the*

Genealogy of Morals—as a master class in the art of rhetoric. In the *Daybreak* rendition, the genealogical argument is literally and rhetorically propounded: It is *pounded* through an array of rhetorical weapons among which the IEDs of hyperbole, satire, parody, and irony feature prominently, while the *pro* is covertly executed through the aforementioned incremental and cumulative method of argumentation whereby successive aphorisms build up 'evidence' in support of a particular proposition. The proposition in question is Nietzsche's genealogical claim that morality is no more than obedience to custom and tradition. As discussed in the chapter's first section, Nietzsche's genealogical claim is so heavily skewed against tradition as to afford a textbook example of the logical fallacy of stacking the deck. The chapter's middle section draws out the text's "involuntary biography" of its author's suffering soul, cf. Zarathustra's maxim, "Write with blood, and you will experience that blood is spirit" (ZI 'On Reading and Writing,' KSA 4:48). And in the third and final section, Nietzsche's penchant for stereotyping is brought to the fore, setting the stage for Chap. 4's sustained critique of BGE's rogues' gallery of 'herd,' 'slave,' and 'rabble' types.

Chapter 4 has a twofold aim. On the one hand, it seeks to challenge the 'perspectivist' approach to Nietzsche's work by confronting BGE's core postulate of an "unalterable, inborn order of rank [*Rangordnung*]" (BGE 263, KSA 5:263). And on the other hand, it seeks to expose the equally unalterable "spiritual *fatum*" of deep-seated prejudices (BGE 231, KSA 5:170) underpinning that postulate and to which (i.e., both the prejudices and the postulate) Nietzsche accords epistemic privilege. The noun '*Rangordnung*' appears more times—seventeen, to be precise—in BGE than it does in any of Nietzsche's other published works. It occurs several times in both volumes of *Human*. But whereas in the latter text it denotes a "spiritual order of rank" (AOM 362, KSA 2:523), or an "order of rank of desirable things [*der Güter*] and of morality" (HH 42, KSA 2:65), in the former it denotes something innate and therefore fixed. The chapter is divided into three sections, each of which illuminates the particular rhetorical strategies deployed by Nietzsche to affirm and adduce his *Rangordnung* claim. The first section provides a detailed exposition and critique of the text's adjectival epithets 'common,' 'herd,' and 'slave,' together with their corresponding compound nouns such as 'herd-men,' 'herd-instinct,' and 'herd-morality,' by means of which Nietzsche classifies and essentializes 'ignoble' ranks and types. The second section draws attention to the text's ambiguous use of the word 'blood' and of the verb '*züchten*,' meaning to breed, grow, or cultivate. The final section highlights the text's emphatically unambiguous use of the adjectives 'fundamental,' 'natural,' 'instinctive,' and 'degenerate.'

Chapter 5 reads *Twilight* against BGE to reveal a shift in tone from the vitriol of the earlier text to the good-natured, light-hearted chaffing of the later work, despite *Twilight*'s subtitle 'How to Philosophize with a Hammer' and despite the text's closing injunction—borrowed from the pity-hobbled Zarathustra—to "*become hard!*" (Z3 'On Old and New Law Tables' 29, KSA 4:268). Thus, while Nietzsche's rhetorical arsenal is still in combat mode, his objective is no longer to slash and burn but to jape and jibe. A glaring exception to this tonal shift is 'The Problem of Socrates,' an early *Twilight* chapter in which Socrates' ugliness precipitates a return to the arguably ugly animus of BGE. Chap. 5 is divided into two halves: The first maps out Nietzsche's path from the malice of BGE to the magnanimity of *Twilight*, while the second examines the philological bad faith in Nietzsche's elaborate attempts to prove that Socrates was a decadent.

In sum, what some Nietzsche commentators dismiss as innocuous rhetorical exuberance, or others celebrate as an invitation to the reader to play, dance, or self-reflect, will in the following case studies be seen as a sophistical style of writing whereby the reader is seduced into giving greater credence to propositions than they would otherwise warrant. By uncovering some of the more prominent rhetorical strategies in Nietzsche's consummate art of persuasion, this book is designed to encourage both novice and expert readers of his work to subject it to the same hermeneutics of suspicion to which Nietzsche fastidiously subjected all philosophical texts, including—if only sporadically—his own. As Nietzsche exhorts us in his preface to *Daybreak*, "*learn* to read me well!"—an art, he explains, that requires one "to read slowly, deeply, looking cautiously fore and aft, with reservations, with doors left open, with delicate eyes and fingers" (D Pref. 5, KSA 3:17).

REFERENCES

Allison, David B. 2001. *Reading the New Nietzsche: The Birth of Tragedy, The Gay Science, Thus Spoke Zarathustra, and On the Genealogy of Morals*. Lanham: Rowman & Littlefield.

Babich, Babette E. 2006. *Words in Blood, Like Flowers: Philosophy and Poetry, Music and Eros in Hölderlin, Nietzsche, and Heidegger*. Albany: SUNY Press.

Blass, Friedrich. 1865. *Die griechische Beredsamkeit in dem Zeitraum von Alexander bis auf Augustus*. 3 vols. Berlin: Weidmann.

Dannhauser, Werner J. 1974. *Nietzsche's View of Socrates*. New York: Cornell University Press.

Gerber, Gustav. 1872. *Die Sprache als Kunst*. Bromberg: Mittler'sche Buchhandlung.

Gilman, Sander L., Carol Blair, and David J. Parent, eds. 1989. *Friedrich Nietzsche on Rhetoric and Language*. New York: Oxford University Press.

Kant, Immanuel. 1961. *The Critique of Judgement*. Trans. James Creed Meredith. Oxford: Clarendon Press.

Kaufmann, Walter. 1974. *Nietzsche: Philosopher, Psychologist, Antichrist*. Princeton: Princeton University Press.

Kofman, Sarah. 1993. *Nietzsche and Metaphor*. Trans. Duncan Large. London: The Athlone Press. Original edition: 1972. *Nietzsche et la métaphore*. Paris: Payot.

Lambek, Simon. 2020. Nietzsche's rhetoric: Dissonance and reception. *Epoché* 25 (1): 57–80.

Magnus, Bernd, Stanley Stewart, and Jean-Pierre Mileur. 1993. *Nietzsche's Case: Philosophy as/and Literature*. New York: Routledge.

Man, Paul de. 1979. *Allegories of Reading: Figural Language in Rousseau, Nietzsche, Rilke, and Proust*. New Haven: Yale University Press.

Nehamas, Alexander. 1985. *Nietzsche: Life as Literature*. Cambridge: Harvard University Press.

Nietzsche, Friedrich. 1992. *Philosophy and Truth: Selections from Nietzsche's Notebooks of the Early 1870's*. Trans. Daniel Breazeale. Atlantic Highlands: Humanities Press.

———. 2002. *Beyond Good and Evil: Prelude to a Philosophy of the Future*. Trans. Judith Norman. Cambridge: Cambridge University Press.

———. 2006a. *Daybreak: Thoughts on the Prejudices of Morality*. Trans. R. J. Hollingdale. Cambridge: Cambridge University Press.

———. 2006b. *The Anti-Christ, Ecce Homo, Twilight of the Idols, and Other Writings*. Trans. Judith Norman. New York: Cambridge University Press.

———. 2007. *Human, All Too Human; A Book for Free Spirits*. Trans. R. J. Hollingdale. Cambridge: Cambridge University Press.

Schopenhauer, Arthur. 1966. *The World as Will and Representation*. Vol. 2. Trans. E. F. J. Payne. New York: Dover.

Schrift, Alan D. 1990. *Nietzsche and the Question of Interpretation: Between Hermeneutics and Deconstruction*. London: Routledge.

Staten, Henry. 1990. *Nietzsche's Voice*. New York: Cornell University Press.

Strong, Tracy B. 2013. In defense of rhetoric: Or how hard it is to take a writer seriously: The case of Nietzsche. *Political Theory* 41 (4): 507–532.

Volkmann, Richard. 1872. *Die Rhetorik der Griechen und Römer in systematischer Übersicht dargestellt*. Berlin: Ebeling and Plahn.

CHAPTER 2

Gnats, Spiders, and Not So "Clever Beasts"

'On Truth and Lies in a Nonmoral Sense' (1873)

Abstract This chapter offers Nietzsche's early, unpublished essay 'On Truth and Lies in a Nonmoral Sense' as a template of his subsequent rhetorical style. A close examination of the text's use of similes, epithets, repetition, wordplay, assonance, and hyperbole will disclose, on the one hand, the rhetorical strategies by means of which Nietzsche polemically transposes the Kantian transcendental aesthetic into a moral harangue on truth and lies, arrogance and ignorance, and on the other hand, how this heightened transposition mirrors the formation of language as expounded by Nietzsche in the essay. According to the latter exposition, language is merely the end product of a series of metaphorical transpositions from sensation to image to sound; it thus lacks the authority to deliver logical, philosophical, or scientific truths. Such 'truths,' therefore, are false, but which Nietzsche rhetorically and moralistically magnifies into 'lies' begotten by human pride, arrogance, and deception. As the chapter points out, Nietzsche's use of such morally freighted terms in his re-staging of Kant's epistemological Copernican revolution incongruously belies the 'nonmoral sense' of truth and lies adverted to in the essay's title, thereby furnishing an early example of the kind of titular-textual misalignment also found in *Twilight* (see Chap. 5).

Keywords Nietzsche • 'Truth and Lies' • Kant • Transcendental idealism • Metaphor • Language

© The Author(s), under exclusive license to Springer Nature Switzerland AG 2023
F. Cauchi, *Nietzsche's Rhetoric*,
https://doi.org/10.1007/978-3-031-42964-4_2

13

INTRODUCTION

Strip away the rhetoric of Nietzsche's 1873 essay 'Truth and Lies,' and what remains is a highly charged, polemical rendition of Kant's transcendental idealism.[1] In the *Critique of Pure Reason* (1781), Kant holds that man's experience of the world is not of 'things in themselves' but only of the appearance of things and that these things *appear* within space and time, which in turn are merely subjective forms of human intuition. These two premises constitute the bedrock of what Kant termed 'transcendental idealism'; they also underpin 'Truth and Lies.'[2] See, for example, Nietzsche's wry observation towards the end of the essay that the same person who recognizes the "contradictory impossibility" of true or correct perception, given the "absolutely different spheres" of subject and object, will nevertheless have "clearly convinced himself of the eternal consistency, omnipresence, and infallibility of the laws of nature." As Nietzsche had learned from Kant (*Critique of Pure Reason*, A125), and also from Schopenhauer's critique of Kant (*The World as Will and Representation*,

---

[1] Lacoue-Labarthe (1993, 25) makes a similar point, noting Nietzsche's wish to "radicalize Kant … [and] his efforts to reduce as it were the a priori to tropes and the transcendental to a fact of language." For a book-length account of Nietzsche's debt to Kant, see Hill (2003). For a reading of the affinities between the Kantian rational will and Zarathustra's doctrine of self-overcoming, see Cauchi (2022).

[2] Setting aside the debate on whether Nietzsche read Kant in the original or via Schopenhauer and/or Lange, Babich (2006, 8) records an ongoing trend in Nietzsche scholarship to "reduce everything in Nietzsche … to prior sources," a trend that not only "disregards the transformations of style" from one text to another, but also excludes both "the music of poetry" and what Nietzsche regarded as historical reflection. Babich (2006, 24) also reminds us that in his early essay 'Philosophy in the Tragic Age of the Greeks,' Nietzsche criticizes "the very notion of 'original' sources in terms of an importantly hermeneutic contextualization of neighboring influences." Kopp (2013, 447) also calls for a more contextualized approach to Nietzsche—not, however, to dissuade the source-hunters, but to correct the continued critical blindness towards the intertextual background of 'Truth and Lies.' It is to this blindness that Kopp attributes Nietzsche's prevailing "monumental status" within the field of rhetoric and writing studies. Kopp himself points to the presence of Schopenhauer in the 1873 essay, while in the late 1980s and early '90s it was Gustav Gerber's *Die Sprache als Kunst* [*Language as Art*] that scholars were citing as a key source of 'Truth and Lies.' For a detailed account of Nietzsche's familiarity with Gerber's *Die Sprache als Kunst*, but also of how Nietzsche's reflections on rhetoric "take him far beyond Gerber," see Porter (1994, 229).

vol. 1, §27), these laws of nature are but human fictions.[3] "[I]f each of us had a different kind of sense-perception," writes Nietzsche in 'Truth and Lies,' "if we could only perceive things now as a bird, now as a worm, now as a plant ... then no one would speak of such a regularity of nature; rather, nature would be grasped only as a creation which is subjective in the highest degree." He goes on to remind us that all we actually know about these so-called laws of nature is "what we ourselves bring to them— time and space, and therefore relationships of succession and number"—a clear iteration of Kant's transcendental aesthetic. Thus, Nietzsche continues, "the mathematical strictness and inviolability of our representations of time and space" are no more than constructs of the human intellect: "we produce these representations in and from ourselves with the same necessity with which the spider spins" (TL 86–87, KSA 1:884–885).[4]

In marked contrast to the relatively flat, expository tenor of the Kantian-inflected statements cited above, Nietzsche's rhetoric in the early part of the essay transforms Kant's transcendental aesthetic into a dual polemic on truth and lies, and on arrogance and ignorance. In choosing such morally freighted terms to re-stage Kant's epistemological Copernican revolution, Nietzsche arguably contradicts the 'nonmoral sense' of the essay's title, a contradiction that will be explored in the first headed section of this chapter. I shall also illustrate how Nietzsche wittingly adopts the same method by which, on his showing, man arrives at his 'truth' claims about the

---

[3] "[T]he order and regularity in ... appearances [i.e. the merely empirical elements of experience], which we entitle *nature*, we ourselves introduce. We could never find them in appearances, had not we ourselves, or the nature of our mind, originally set them there" (*CPR*, A125). "[I]n the school of Schelling we find, among their many different efforts to bring to light the analogy between all the phenomena of nature, many attempts, although unfortunate ones, to derive laws of nature from the mere laws of space and time" (*WWR* I:27). See also Kopp (2013), cited in the preceding footnote.

[4] It is important, here, that Anglophone readers are not misled by a false idiomatic friend, namely Sir Walter Scott's couplet from his epic poem *Marmion: A Tale of Flodden Field*, "Oh, what a tangled web we weave/When first we practice to deceive." For while the core argument of Nietzsche's essay is that the human intellect's all-too-human re-presentations of the phenomenal world are 'lies,' they are not witting lies but rather the product of natural necessity. It is this unwittingness which throws into incongruous relief Nietzsche's moralistic attacks on these representational 'lies' (to be discussed in the course of this chapter). The spider's web imagery evokes the somewhat comical image of man getting caught (up), unlike the spider, in his own representational web—an analogy which, like so many of Nietzsche's other animal analogies in the essay, is deployed with the intention of ridiculing man's pride in being the superior animal on earth.

world, namely, by rhetorically heightening, transposing, and embellishing (TL 84, KSA 1:880).[5] The first of these rhetorical practices can be seen not only in the aforesaid moral diction, but in Nietzsche's heavily loaded similes. One of these similes is the spider's web—a web that ensnares in much the same way as Nietzsche's intricate rhetorical web ensnares the reader: Just as the first immobilizes the insect's flight, the second immobilizes the reader's critical judgment.

A typical example of Nietzsche's tendentious comparisons can be found in the essay's opening paragraph. Here, he mockingly compares man's unquestioning belief in the truth of the human mind's representations of the phenomenal world to, on the one hand, the pre-Copernican belief that the earth is the center of the universe and on the other hand, to what Nietzsche confidently asserts is the gnat's sense of the world. If we could but communicate with the gnat, he muses, we would discover that it too "feels the flying center of the universe within itself" (TL 79, KSA 1:875). What is being rhetorically heightened here is man's misplaced pride in human knowledge, an inflated self-importance summarily deflated by the gnat analogy. Later in the essay, Nietzsche employs two more insect analogies and with the same derisory objective. In the first, the logician is compared to the spider: Just as the former, whom "one may certainly admire as a mighty genius of construction," successfully piles up "an infinitely complicated dome of concepts upon an unstable foundation and, as it were, on running water," so the spider's web is delicate enough to be carried along by the waves but strong enough not to be blown asunder by each gust of wind (TL 85, KSA 1:882). Derision oozes out of the ironic epithet "mighty genius" and the equally ironic admiration for an edifice ludicrously built on unsound foundations. In the second insect analogy, Nietzsche draws a comparison between the worker bee and the scientist: Just as the former busily constructs cells and fills them up with honey, the latter works tirelessly within a "monstrously towering framework" of concepts and accommodates within it "the entire empirical world, which is to say, the anthropomorphic world" (TL 88, KSA 1:886). One might also add that whereas the bee's honey is sweet and nutritious, the scientist's conceptual schemata is as dry as dust.

[5] Indeed, as Hillis Miller (1981, 46) remarks on Nietzsche's use of "proliferating metaphors" in 'Truth and Lies,' "That he must use what he condemns is evident, since language, as Nietzsche sees it, is either made of overt metaphors or of those frozen and effaced tropes he calls concepts."

Another arresting simile in the essay is the Roman columbarium, whose "rigid regularity" Nietzsche compares to logic's air of "strength and coolness characteristic of mathematics,"[6] despite the artificial nature of language. As expounded by Nietzsche in the essay, language originates in a nerve stimulus, which is subsequently transposed into three consecutive, substitutive metaphors: perceptual (image), verbal (sound), and conceptual (abstraction). These metaphors, moreover, are merely the "*residue of a metaphor*" (emphasis in the original)—fossilized impressions which remain after the vivid first impression (sensation) has been serially transposed and ultimately etherealized [*verflüchtigen*] into a concept (TL 84–85, KSA 1:881–882). And just as the funerary urns in a Roman columbarium contain the residue of the person cremated, so the abstract concepts with which scientists, logicians, and philosophers ply their trade represent "the graveyard of perceptions" (TL 88, KSA 1:886).

Nietzsche's similes need to be read with caution. For if the spider's web, the honeycomb, and the Roman columbarium are all remarkably apt similes,[7] the false equivalence between gnats and "clever beast" philosophers, scientists, and logicians is palpably tendentious. In Chap. 3 of this study, I shall cite further instances of false equivalence, but instances which have far more serious implications for Nietzsche's philosophical claims than his mischievous gnat simile.

TRUTH AND LIES IN A MORAL SENSE

Nietzsche's unfinished, posthumously published essay 'Truth and Lies' is divided into two sections, the first of which is twice the length of the second. Nietzsche's dual objective in the first is to diminish and admonish man's vaunted view of his intellectual powers. This objective is epitomized in the opening sentence's 'clever beast' epithet and is thereafter tactically pursued by the deployment of four rhetorical weapons: deck-stacking, hyperbole, moral condemnation, and false equivalence. I shall begin with

---

[6] In *Twilight*, Nietzsche deploys the homonyms '*Zeichenlehre*' [a theory of signs] and '*Zeichenlehrer*' [art teacher] to argue that logic and mathematics are merely art forms: "In these formal sciences, reality makes no appearance at all, not even as a problem; nor is there any hint of the question of what value such a convention of signs has in the first place" (TI "Reason" 3, KSA 6:76).

[7] For an in-depth reading of these three images, see Kofman (1993, 61–73).

deck-stacking and hyperbole,[8] both of which are evident in Nietzsche's characterization of the human intellect as "pitiful … shadowy and fleeting … useless and arbitrary," and a relatively late arrival in the history of the universe. Accordingly, "when it is all over with the human intellect, nothing will have happened" (TL 79, KSA 1:875), since its claims to knowledge are ineluctably human. By 'human intellect,' Nietzsche means an intellect that can only ever register impressions received via the five portals of human sensation and produce from these impressions anthropomorphic representations of the empirical world in which man finds himself—in short, Kantian transcendental idealism. Far from being an accurate copy of the thing sensed or perceived, these representations, polemicizes Nietzsche, are merely illusions masquerading as empirical truths: "Truths are illusions which we have forgotten are illusions" (TL 84, KSA 1:880–881). To add insult to injury, which nicely encapsulates the essay's rhetorical thrust, the human intellect—as pitiful as it is—is the one that has been allotted to those "most unfortunate, delicate, and ephemeral beings" (more deck-stacking) as a tool for deceiving them as to the value of their transient existence. It also serves as a ruse for detaining them in that existence "for only a minute" (TL 79, KSA 1:876)—note Nietzsche's exaggerated foreshortening of the human life-span.

Another key rhetorical weapon in the essay's human belittlement campaign is moral censure—a distinctly odd tactical maneuver given the essay's title and one that produces the same kind of titular-textual misalignment to be met with in Nietzsche's much later work, *Twilight* (to be discussed in Chap. 5). The 'nonmoral sense' of the titular 'truth and lies' refers to the fundamentally deceptive nature of human knowledge, which man takes to be a truthful (accurate, mimetic) representation of reality. But in the essay's opening two sentences, human "knowing" is said to be not only an "invention," but "the most arrogant [*hochmüchtig*] and mendacious [*verlogen*] minute of 'world-history'" (TL 79, KSA 1:876). The adjective '*verlogen*,' derived from the root word '*Lüge*,' meaning lie or falsehood, is the essay's first allusion to the titular—and morally loaded—'lies.' For if these allegedly, but oxymoronic-sounding, 'nonmoral' lies are

---

[8] According to Nehamas (1985, 22 & 28, respectively), hyperbole is the "single most pervasive feature" of Nietzsche's writing from *The Birth of Tragedy* through to *Ecce Homo*. Whether the effect of this traditional rhetorical figure on the Nietzsche reader is attraction, repulsion, or blank incomprehension, it is one which never fails to make an impression: "The one reaction Nietzsche cannot tolerate is indifference, and this is what his use of hyperbole is designed to eliminate."

simply intended to denote the false coinage of the human intellect, or what Nietzsche in *Twilight* refers to as "the prejudice of reason" (TI "Reason" 5, KSA 6:77), the transferred epithets 'arrogant' and 'mendacious' flatly contradict the 'nonmoral' qualifier, not least because '*verlogen*' hints at the witting deception of those who claim to 'know.' More curious still, these two epithets undermine the essay's subsequent portrayal of man as one who is "deeply immersed in illusions and dream images" (TL 80, KSA 1:876), a prisoner and dupe of his own nature. Hence Nietzsche's withering contempt for the philosopher, "the proudest of men," whom he radically cuts down to size by comparing him to a gnat: Just as the most "despicable and insignificant" of creatures would "immediately swell up like a balloon [*Schlauch*] at the slightest puff [*Anhauch*] of this power of knowing," so the philosopher "supposes that he sees on all sides the eyes of the universe telescopically focused upon his action and thought" (TL 79, KSA 1:875–876). It is precisely this pre-Copernican-like self-aggrandizement, underscored by the rhyming nouns '*Schlauch*' and '*Anhauch*,' that Nietzsche 'telescopically' inverts at the start of the essay with his once-upon-a-time "fable" about a distant star (Earth), "in a remote corner of the universe," upon which some "clever beasts invented knowing" (TL 79, KSA 1:875).

The gentle derision of the essay's first paragraph is followed in the second by robust moral censure:

> The arrogance [*Hochmut*] connected [*verbunden*] with knowing and sensing lies like a blinding [*verblenden*] fog over the eyes and senses of men, thus deceiving [*täuschen*] them concerning the value of existence. For this arrogance contains within itself the most flattering estimation of the value of knowing. Deception [*Täuschung*] is the most general effect of such arrogance, but even its most particular effects contain within themselves something of the same deceitful character. (TL 80, KSA 1:876)

In this passage, we find clear traces of Nietzsche's moral and philological training, exhibited here in his references to arrogance, deceitfulness, and flattering self-estimation, and in his keen eye for wordplay (paronomasia). As Aristotle tells us, homonyms do the sophists' "dirty work" (2007, 200), a covert strategy that subtly imbues rather than hammers home. Here, the verb '*verbunden*' means both to connect and to bandage. By surreptitiously linking the second meaning to the verb '*verblenden*,' meaning to blind, Nietzsche uses the homonymous pair to reinforce the causal link he is seeking to forge between arrogance and the blindfold effect of self-deception. He then heightens the rhetorical effect by freighting arrogance with vanity via the collocation "flattering estimation."[9]

In the third paragraph, however, Nietzsche ups the rhetorical ante by unleashing a barrage of moral condemnation. He begins with the relatively innocuous deck-stacking observation that the intellect "unfolds its *principal* powers in dissimulation"[10] as a means of preserving the *"weaker, less robust* individuals" (my emphasis). In lieu of horns or flesh-tearing teeth, the weaker individuals have no option but to rely on their wits for self-preservation. Thus it is that the human animal looks to the intellect to teach it the art of subterfuge.[11]

> This art of dissimulation [*Verstellungskunst*] reaches its peak in man. Hoodwinking, flattering [*Schmeicheln*], lying and deceiving [*Lügen und Trügen*], talking behind backs [*Hinter-dem-Rücken-Reden*], putting up a false front, living in borrowed splendor, wearing a mask, hiding behind convention [*verhüllende Convention*], playing a role [*Bühnenspiel*] for others and for oneself—in short, a continuous fluttering around the solitary flame of vanity [*das fortwährende Herumflattern um die eine Flamme Eitelkeit*]— is so much the rule and the law among men that there is almost nothing which is less comprehensible than how an honest and pure drive for truth could have arisen among them. They are deeply immersed in illusions and in

---

[9] Nietzsche's tethering of vanity to the "arrogance" of knowing brings out another correspondence between Nietzsche and Kant. As Downard (2004, 1–2) observes, both Kant and Nietzsche hold empiricists and rationalists to be in error and for roughly the same reason. According to Kant, empiricist and rationalist accounts of morality are mistaken because they ground morality in a principle of self-love rather than in a pure (i.e., not motivated by self-interest) incentive of respect (for moral reasons). And according to Nietzsche, empiricists and rationalists are mistaken in attempting to ground their accounts of truth in vanity rather than in a pure love of truth. Downward cites the following lines from 'Truth and Lies,' "[vanity] is so much the rule and the law among men that there is almost nothing which is less comprehensible than how an honest and pure drive for truth could have arisen among them," which he glosses (correctly in my view) as follows: "Our thinking can only express our status as free beings if the impulse to truth, or to any end for that matter, is a pure impulse."

[10] Lacoue-Labarthe (1993, 25) astutely observes that *Verstellung*, the art of dissimulation, "is the very perversion of *Vorstellung*, of representation."

[11] Nietzsche may well have had in mind here the way in which the weaker animals instinctively resort to mimicry and camouflage.

dream images; their eyes merely glide over the surface of things and see "forms." (TL 80, KSA 1:876)

Aside from the moral invective, what is most striking about the above passage is the blatant conflation of the moral (voluntary) and the epistemological (involuntary): on the one hand, human vanity and duplicity, and on the other hand, the inescapably human aspect of human knowing (the Kantian transcendental aesthetic). Thus, while the title of the essay puts the reader on notice that the moral binary 'truth and lies' will be used 'in a nonmoral sense,' the same moral binary underpins the above block quotation, aided and abetted by the rhyming and chiming of *Lügen und Trügen*, *verhüllen* and *Bühnen*, and the two pairs of assonance, *flattern/ Flamme* and *eine/Eitelkeit*, in the hyperbolic phrase "a constant fluttering around the single flame of vanity."
Nietzsche continues:

Their senses nowhere lead to truth; on the contrary, they are content [*beg- nügen sich*] to receive stimuli and, as it were, to engage in a groping game on the backs of things. Moreover, man permits himself [*lassen sich*] to be deceived in his dreams every night of his life. His moral sentiment [*mor- alisches Gefühl*] does not even make an attempt to prevent this, whereas there are supposed to be men who have stopped snoring through sheer will power. (TL 80, KSA 1:876–877)

The moral condemnation is more muted here, but is implicit in the reflexive verbs '*begnügen sich*' and '*lassen sich*.' Despite the fact that the human senses, steeped as they are in "illusions and dream images," are powerless to alter the way in which they receive stimuli, they are personified and judged for being "content" with this state of affairs. Censure is also implicit in the equally absurd suggestion that one should try to prevent the "deceit" that governs our nocturnal dreams. Further disapproval can be heard in the grubby-sounding "groping game" that man is content to play "on the backs of things [*Rücken der Dinge*]"—the repetition of *Rücken* subtly recuperating the dirty laundry list of dissimulation that had included talking behind backs [*Hinter-dem-Rücken-Reden*] and hiding behind masks and mores. Militating against these moral judgments, however, is Nietzsche's acknowledgment, made in the same paragraph, that man is an involuntary victim of his own nature. Not only does nature conspire to keep man aloof from his blood and bowels "in order to confine and lock him within a proud, deceptive consciousness ... She [i.e., nature] threw away the key." Notwithstanding this acknowledgment, followed by Nietzsche's dire warning against "that fatal curiosity which might one day have the power to peer out and down through a crack in the chamber of consciousness," the third paragraph concludes with a veiled reproach ("nonchalance") and another reminder of man's bestial provenance ("tiger"). Man, we are told, is "sustained in the nonchalance of his ignorance by that which is pitiless, greedy, insatiable, and murderous—as if hanging in dreams on the back of a tiger" (TL 80, KSA 1:877). Note the stark contrast between man's predatory drives and his blithely ignorant consciousness, the blindness of the latter proving easy prey for the inexorable will of the former.

What are we to make of this moralization of the Kantian transcendental aesthetic? First, it is important to register the essay's tacit endorsement of Kant's account of the *ineluctably* human quality of all concepts generated by the human mind. Second, Nietzsche's moral indignation at the vanity and misplaced pride of the 'clever beast' philosophers in the veracity of their truth claims ought to give the reader serious pause when encountering the ostensibly nonmoral stance of Nietzsche's avowedly 'immoralist' philosophy. An outstanding example of the moralism underpinning Nietzsche's celebrated immoralism is his objection in *Human* to the "pitying, benevolent impulses" of the 'good' Christian, which he simultaneously juxtaposes to his preference for "a continual self-command and self-overcoming practiced in great things and in the smallest" (WS 45, KSA 2:573–574)—the type of self-conquest and self-discipline, moreover, that he explicitly admires in the Jesuit priest (HH 55, KSA 2:74–75). Third, the moral tenor of his 'truth and lies' rhetoric should not be dismissed as mere rhetoric. As I have sought to demonstrate above, Nietzsche's rhetoric is the vehicle through which he not only advances his philosophical claims but also, be it consciously or unconsciously, contradicts them.

SHELTERING UNDER THE BULWARK
OF "GHOSTLY SCHEMATA"

In this section, I shall highlight three further rhetorical strategies in 'Truth and Lies,' with a view to preparing the reader for their equally tendentious use in *Daybreak*. These three strategies are the use of triadic and/or homonymous patterns of argumentation and the use of repetition. The first two devices are deployed in the essay to shore up the proposition (1) that the language-creator's [*Sprachbildner*] belief in a correspondence theory of truth is an illusion, while the second and third devices are used to support the proposition (2) that these fabricated laws of truth serve not just an individual's need for self-preservation but society's also.

Regarding proposition (1), Nietzsche asserts that the "first laws of truth" [*Gesetze der Warheit*] were established by the language-creator's invention of a "uniformly valid and binding designation of things [*verbindlich Bezeichnung der Dinge*]"—in other words, a de facto "legislation of language" [*Gesetzgebung der Sprache*] (TL 80, KSA 1:877). Note the serial progression from an invented designation of things to legislation and truth, marked here by the triad *der Dinge—der Sprache—der Wahrheit*. Nietzsche uses the same device in the essay's opening analogy between the philosopher and the gnat and with the same rhetorical objective, namely to expose, deride and censure man's proud claims to knowledge. If we could but communicate [*verständigen*] with the gnat, which (according to Nietzsche) feels itself to be the airborne omphalos of the universe, we would learn [*vernehmen*] that even the smallest, most despicable [*verwerflich*] of creatures would swell with the pride of knowing. And although man's girth is considerably larger than that of the gnat, the same cannot be said of the knowledge which fills the philosopher with such pride,

> If I make up the definition of a mammal, and then, after inspecting a camel, declare "Look, a mammal," I have indeed brought a truth to light in this way, but it is a truth of limited value. That is to say, it is a thoroughly anthropomorphic truth which contains not a single point which would be "true in itself" or really and universally valid apart from man. (TL 85, KSA 1:883)

Note, once again, the moral attack on human pride, delivered here through the third term in the *verständigen—vernehmen—verwerflich* triad. Note, too, Nietzsche's use of the rhetorical figure of dialogue, to be discussed at greater length in Chap. 5.

Regarding proposition (2), namely that the *Sprachbildner's* laws of truth preserve social cohesion, these laws—held by Nietzsche to be "linguistic conventions" masquerading as "adequate expression[s] of reality"—decree that the word 'liar' will apply to anyone who uses the coined designations as false coinage. Under this dispensation, the liar will be ostracized from society for violating in a "selfish" or "harmful" manner the "fixed conventions by means of arbitrary substitutions." But as Nietzsche points out, the expulsion is due less to the deception [*Betrogenwerden*] than to the injury sustained [*Beschädigtwerden*], i.e., "the unpleasant, hated consequences of certain sorts of deception" (TL 81, KSA 1:877–878). Note here Nietzsche's double irony: First, that the "fixed conventions" violated by the liar's arbitrary substitutions are themselves arbitrary, and second, that the liar's exclusion from society on account of the lie's harmful consequences to society is no less selfish—i.e., a desire to avoid further harm—than the selfish motives prompting the liar's illegitimate usage. Note, too, the staged, quasi-homonymous opposition between '*Betrogenwerden*' (being deceived) and '*Beschädigtwerden*' (being injured), underscoring man and society's fundamental drive towards self-preservation.

This need for self-preservation is also emphasized in the essay through the use of repetition, the third rhetorical strategy in focus here. According to Nietzsche, the greatest linguistic lie of the *Sprachbildner* is its "great edifice of concepts" (TL 85, KSA 1:882), under the bulwark of which man and society gather in the shared interest of self-preservation: "man wishes to exist socially and with the herd" (TL 81, KSA 1:877). This self-preservative need is indexed in the first half of the essay by the repeated use of both the reflexive pronoun *sich* and the adverbial limiting modifier *only*. I shall deal with each in turn.

Two successive paragraphs open with the claim that the principal powers of the human intellect are employed in protecting the individual from other individuals. Whether in a state of nature or in society, man's overriding concern is to "save himself [*sich retten*]" (TL 90, KSA 1:888), and the most effective method of doing so, argues Nietzsche, is by forgetting that man is "an *artistically creating* subject" (TL 86, KSA 1:883). Only by forgetting this fact can the individual live with any "repose, security [*Sicherheit*], and consistency [*Consequenz*]" (ibid.)—a point which is repeated in three contiguous paragraphs and buttressed by the reflexive pronoun. In the first of these paragraphs, Nietzsche wryly observes how the scientific investigator has

> clearly convinced himself [*sich überzeugen*] of the eternal consistency [*Consequenz*], omnipresence, and infallibility of the laws of nature. He has concluded that so far as we can penetrate here—from the telescopic heights to the microscopic depths—everything is secure [*sicher*], complete, infinite, regular, and without any gaps. (TL 87, KSA 1:885)

Note, once again, Nietzsche's ironic reference to skewed optics, the "telescopic heights and microscopic depths" hinting at the magnitude of the scientist's self-deception concerning the "infallibility" of the laws of nature. In the second of these paragraphs, we are told that even the man of action relies upon reason and concepts so as not to be swept away and lose himself [*sich verlieren*] (TL 88, KSA 1:886). And again, towards the end of the essay, the *Sprachbildner*'s immense conceptual framework is said to be that to which "the needy man clings his whole life long in order to save himself [*sich retten*]" (TL 90, KSA 1:888).

The sheer scale of this conceptual deception is impressed upon the reader through the repetition of the noun 'metaphor' and the limiting modifier 'only.' The former can be found in the following passage, where it is used to reinforce the dual argument that "every concept is only the *residue of a metaphor*" (TL 85, KSA 1:882) and that neither concept nor metaphor bears an accurate relation to the object 'in itself.'

> [The language-creator] only designates the relations of things to men, and for expressing these relations he lays hold of the boldest metaphors. To begin with, a nerve stimulus is transferred into an image: first metaphor. The image, in turn, is imitated in a sound: second metaphor. And each time there is a complete overleaping of one sphere, right into the middle of an entirely new and different sphere ... It is this way with all of us concerning language: we believe that we know something about the things themselves when we speak of trees, colors, snow, and flowers; and yet we possess nothing but metaphors for things—[metaphors] which correspond in no way to the original entities. (TL 82-3, KSA 1:879)

As noted above, it is *only* by forgetting that the original perceptual meta-phors are indeed metaphors that, on Nietzsche's showing, man is able to live with any sense of security and consistency.

This brings us to Nietzsche's use of the limiting modifier 'only,' a veri-table battalion of which are deployed by him in two successive paragraphs. In the first of these, the rhetorical target is the aforementioned correspon-dence theory of truth:

> Only by forgetting this primitive world of metaphor ... only by means of the petrification and coagulation of a mass of images which originally streamed from the primal faculty of human imagination like a fiery liquid, only in the invincible faith that *this* sun, *this* window, *this* table is a truth in itself, in short, only by forgetting that he himself is an *artistically creating* subject, does man live with any repose, security, and consistency. If but for an instant he could escape from the prison walls of this faith, his "self-consciousness" would be immediately destroyed. (TL 86, KSA 1:883)

Not content, however, with having breached the fortifications of man's faith in language, Nietzsche re-deploys the limiting modifier in the imme-diately succeeding paragraph in a bid to lay waste to man's firm belief in the laws of nature. Armed with the Kantian insight that space and time constitute the framework within which the human mind constructs its experience of reality, the ever-serviceable modifier is duly dispatched:

> if we could only perceive things now as a bird, now as a worm, now as a plant ... nature would be grasped only as a creation which is subjective in the highest degree. After all, what is a law of nature as such for us? We are not acquainted with it in itself, but only with its effects ... which, in turn, are known to us only as sums of relations. Therefore, all these relations only ever refer again to others and are thoroughly incomprehensible to us in their essence; only what we add to them, time and space, and therefore relation-ships of succession and number, are really known to us. But everything mar-velous about the laws of nature ... lies only and entirely in the mathematical rigor and inviolability of our representations of time and space ... If we are forced to comprehend all things only under these forms, then it ceases to be amazing that we really only understand all things under these forms ... The only way in which the possibility of subsequently constructing a new con-ceptual edifice from metaphors themselves can be explained is by the firm persistence of these original forms. (TL 87-8, KSA 1:885-886)

Nietzsche ends the essay by setting the rational man and the intuitive man side by side. While both seek to rule over life, the "foresight, prudence, and regularity" of the former is juxtaposed to "the most audacious feats" of the latter. Liberated from the straitjacket of concepts and guided solely by intuition, the creative mind "smashes [the conceptual] framework to pieces ... and puts it back together in an ironic fashion, pairing the most alien things and separating the closest" (TL 90, KSA 1:888–889). This kind of promiscuous pairing is, of course, Nietzsche's principal rhetorical method in 'Truth and Lies.' And as I have tried to show in this chapter, such comparisons are not only ironic, but also moral. Nietzsche's gnat, bee, and spider similes set into relief not just the alleged pride of scientists, logicians, and philosophers, but also their alleged arrogance, ignorance, and vanity. Where, pray tell, is the nonmoral sense of truth and lies?

A STYLISTIC TEMPLATE

Written when Nietzsche was one year shy of his thirtieth birthday, 'Truth and Lies' provides the reader with a template of Nietzsche's rhetorical tics and tactics. In this concluding section, I shall select a few of the devices highlighted above and flag their dubious or self-defeating deployment in the three texts to be examined in the remaining chapters of this study, namely *Daybreak*, BGE, and *Twilight*.

In *Daybreak*, we encounter Nietzsche's predilection for what in Chap. 3 of this monograph I term "adverbial troweling." Whereas in 'Truth and Lies' Nietzsche uses the adverbial modifier 'only' to chip away at the conceptual framework in which man places so much trust and security, in *Daybreak* he uses the adverb '*fortwährend*,' meaning constantly, continually, or perpetually, to exaggerate man's obedience to customs. The caricatured Brahmin is a case in point, *constantly* on the lookout for opportunities to obey the laws of custom that occupy his mind at every minute of every day (D 9, KSA 3:22–23). Another example is a particular species of custom said to be found among barbarous peoples, the sole purpose of which is to keep *constantly* present in the mind of each member of the community both the *constant* proximity of custom and the *perpetual* compulsion to practice these customs (D 16, KSA 3:29). In both cases, the adverbially delivered hyperbole undermines the text's core proposition—that morality is simply obedience to custom—and the genealogical narrative used to anchor that proposition.

In BGE, the use of epithets, particularly the compound epithet, is a distinctive rhetorical feature of the text. As we saw in the case of 'Truth and Lies,' the knower is variously referred to as a "clever beast" [*kluge Tier*], a "language-creator" [*Sprachbildner*], and a "mighty genius of construction" [*Baugenie*], for whom man is the alpha and omega and the measure of all things (TL 86). In BGE, however, the compound epithets serve the specific rhetorical objective of establishing a fixed, two-tier order of rank among human beings, namely, the noble and the ignoble. It is for the latter rank that Nietzsche reserves his most derogatory compound epithets such as "rabble man" [*Pöbelmann*], "rabble type" [*Pöbel-Typus*], and "herd men" [*Heerdenmenschen*], collectively typified by their "herd instincts" [*Heerden-Instinkte*], "herd-morality" [*Heerden-Moral*], and numerous other 'herd'-like qualities. As I shall argue in Chap. 4, the cumulative effect of these ubiquitous compound epithets—a veritable "brick wall" of entrenched prejudices (BGE 231, KSA 5:170)—is to numb the reader's critical faculties such that the essentializing discourse of 'types' and 'instincts' slips under the radar.

In *Twilight*, Nietzsche rehearses two images from 'Truth and Lies.' The first of these images relates to the deadening effect of abstraction. The philosopher's "great edifice of concepts," which in TL is compared to "the rigid regularity of a Roman columbarium," is derided in *Twilight* as a form of mummification, as "Egyptianism" (TI "Reason" 1, KSA 6:74–75). Similarly, just as the Platonic Form or abstract concept of a leaf is said in TL to drain the life, color, and contours out of each individual leaf, so in *Twilight* the "prejudice of reason [*Vernunft-Vorurtheil*]" is said to petrify the flux of life into static concepts of substance, permanence, identity, and so forth (TI "Reason" 5, KSA 6:77). In short, "[t]hey kill and stuff the things they worship, these lords of concept idolatry" (TI "Reason" 1, KSA 6:74). It is important to note, however, that the above-mentioned compound epithets in BGE similarly petrify the flux of life, by classifying and essentializing individuals as slave, herd, or rabble types and by listing these types under a static, "unalterable, inborn order of rank [*eingeborne Rangordnung*]" (BGE 263, KSA 5:263). The second image that appears in both the early essay and *Twilight* is that of the spider's web. In the later text, the concept of *causa sui* is said to be one of the "brainsick fancies of morbid cobweb-spiders" (TI "Reason" 4, KSA 6:76), while in the former, the "infinitely complicated dome of concepts," erected Kubla Khan-like upon the incessant flux of life, is ironically compared to a spider's web—strong enough to withstand a gust of wind but not the force of Nietzsche's withering critique (TL 85, KSA 1:882). But that critique, whether of language and concept builders or of 'herd' and 'slave' types, is also a spider's web. It is an intricate web of metaphors, similes, homonyms, repetition, and other rhetorical ruses—strong enough to entrap the reader but not if we have learned how to read Nietzsche well, i.e., "slowly, deeply, looking cautiously fore and aft, with reservations, with doors left open, with delicate eyes and fingers" (D Pref. 5, KSA 3:17).

Homonyms and assonance are stock in trade for Nietzsche, but they serve a far more important purpose than merely rhetorical theatrics. As noted in the first section of this chapter, Nietzsche uses both devices to forge causal connections between ostensible opposites and to draw arresting parallels between different orders of things. In BGE, the homonymous adjectives 'verderbt' [corrupted] and 'vererbt' [inherited] are used to forge a genetic link between contaminated blood and "inherited vulgarity" [vererbten Pöbel], while the adjectival quartet 'reinlich' [clean], 'unreinlich' [unclean], 'unvermeidlich' [ineluctable], and 'gemein' [common] is proffered as an explanation for and justification of the noble individual's need for solitude. Defined by Nietzsche as "a sublime inclination and impulse to cleanliness," the solitude of the noble translates into an involuntary shrinking from contact with the insalubrious rabble—contact which "must inevitably make things unclean" [unvermeidlich-unreinlich zugehn muss] (BGE 284, KSA 232). Once again, the rhetorical objective here is to essentialize the 'noble' and 'ignoble' types.

Two more devices in Nietzsche's rhetorical arsenal are the symbiotic pair: satire and dialogue. In 'Truth and Lies,' satirical parallels are drawn between man and some of man's least liked insects such as gnats, bees, and spiders. As noted above, the diminutive dimension of these insects serves Nietzsche's rhetorical aim to diminish the human intellect to a dupe of its own nature and a flunky in the service of self-preservation. The essay's opening "fable" about a distant galactic star sets the satirical tone that prevails throughout the essay,

> Once upon a time, in some out of the way corner of that universe which is dispersed into numberless twinkling solar systems, there was a star upon which clever beasts invented knowing. That was the most arrogant and mendacious minute of "world history," but nevertheless, it was only a minute. After nature had drawn a few breaths, the star cooled and congealed, and the clever beasts had to die. (TL 79, KSA 1:875)

We hear the same satirical tone in Nietzsche's straw-man dialogues. Compare, for example, his 'Truth and Lies' caricature (cited above) of reason's delighted 'discovery' of a mammal ("Look, a mammal!")—the definition of which reason has itself invented—with the following *Twilight* caricature of reason's contortions when confronted with its failure to grasp the 'thing in itself.'

> "There has to be an illusion, a deception at work that prevents us from per-ceiving what *is*. Where's the deceiver?"—"We've got the deceiver!" they cry happily. "It's sensation! These senses, *which are so immoral anyway*, deceive us about the *true* world ... [A]way with the *body*, this pathetic *idée fixe* of the senses, afflicted with every logical error there is, refuted, impossible even—although it has the nerve to behave as if it were real!" (TI "Reason" 1, KSA 6:74–75)[12]

In 'The Problem of Socrates' (the second chapter of *Twilight*), however, ventriloquized dialogue is used for darker purposes. In an attempt to prove that Socrates was a declining type, Nietzsche not only has Socrates confess that death for him is a welcome cure for life's ills, but also that he has anarchic instincts commensurate with what a passing physiognomist referred to as Socrates' *monstrum*-like features ('Socrates' 3, KSA 6:69). These two 'confessions' are then used by Nietzsche to forge a link between ugliness and decadence, physiognomy and physiology.

REFERENCES

Aristotle. 2007. In *On Rhetoric: A Theory of Civic Discourse*, ed. George A. Kennedy, 2nd ed. New York: Oxford University Press.
Babich, Babette E. 2006. *Words in Blood, Like Flowers: Philosophy and Poetry, Music and Eros in Hölderlin, Nietzsche, and Heidegger*. Albany: SUNY Press.
Cauchi, Francesca. 2022. *Zarathustra's Moral Tyranny: Spectres of Kant, Hegel and Feuerbach*. Edinburgh: Edinburgh University Press.
Downard, Jeffrey. 2004. Nietzsche and Kant on the pure impulse to truth. *Journal of Nietzsche Studies* 27: 18–41.
Hill, R. Kevin. 2003. *Nietzsche's Critiques: The Kantian Foundations of his Thought*. Oxford: Oxford University Press.

---

[12] Note that the illusion and deception which (Cartesian) reason suspects the senses of perpetrating is a rehearsal of the illusion and deception which in 'Truth and Lies' rational man is said to practice unwittingly on himself.

Hillis Miller, J. 1981. Dismembering and disremembering in Nietzsche's 'On Truth and Lies in a Nonmoral Sense.' *Boundary* 2 (9/10): 41–54.

Kant, Immanuel. 1929. *Critique of Pure Reason*. Trans. Norman Kemp Smith. London: Macmillan.

Kofman, Sarah. 1993. *Nietzsche and Metaphor*. Trans. Duncan Large. London: The Athlone Press. Original edition: 1972. *Nietzsche et la métaphore*. Paris: Payot.

Kopp, Drew. 2013. Nietzsche's teacher: The invisible rhetor. *Rhetoric Review* 32 (4): 437–454.

Lacoue-Labarthe, Phillipe. 1993. *The Subject of Philosophy*. Trans. T. Trezise, H. J. Silverman et al. Minneapolis: University of Minnesota Press.

Nehamas, Alexander. 1985. *Nietzsche: Life as Literature*. Cambridge: Harvard University Press.

Nietzsche, Friedrich. 1992. *Philosophy and Truth: Selections from Nietzsche's Notebooks of the Early 1870's*. Trans. Daniel Breazeale. Atlantic Highlands: Humanities Press.

———. 2002. *Beyond Good and Evil: Prelude to a Philosophy of the Future*. Trans. Judith Norman. Cambridge: Cambridge University Press.

———. 2006a. *Daybreak: Thoughts on the Prejudices of Morality*. Trans. R. J. Hollingdale. Cambridge: Cambridge University Press.

———. 2006b. *The Anti-Christ, Ecce Homo, Twilight of the Idols, and Other Writings*. Trans. Judith Norman. New York: Cambridge University Press.

———. 2007. *Human, All Too Human: A Book for Free Spirits*. Trans. R. J. Hollingdale. Cambridge: Cambridge University Press.

Porter, James I. 1994. Nietzsche's rhetoric: Theory and strategy. *Philosophy & Rhetoric* 27 (3): 218–244.

Schopenhauer, Arthur. 1969. *The World as Will and Representation*, ed. E. F. J. Payne, vol. 1. New York: Dover.

Nietzsche's Rhetorical Arsenal

Daybreak: Thoughts on the Prejudices of Morality (1881)

Abstract In this chapter, Nietzsche's *Daybreak* account of the genealogy of morals—an often overlooked precursor to the later and better known *On the Genealogy of Morals*—is presented as a master class in the art of rhetoric. In the *Daybreak* rendition, the genealogical argument is literally and rhetorically pro-pounded: It is *pounded* through an array of rhetorical weapons among which the IEDs of hyperbole, satire, parody, and irony feature prominently, while the *pro* is covertly executed through an incremental and cumulative method of argumentation whereby successive aphorisms build up 'evidence' in support of a particular proposition. The proposition in question is Nietzsche's genealogical claim that morality is no more than obedience to custom and tradition. But as discussed in the chapter's first section, Nietzsche's genealogical claim is so heavily skewed against tradition as to afford a textbook example of the logical fallacy of stacking the deck. The chapter's middle section draws out the text's "involuntary biography" (D 481, KSA 3:285-286) of its author's suffering soul, cf. Zarathustra's maxim, "Write with blood, and you will experience that blood is spirit" (Z1 'On Reading and Writing,' KSA 4:48). And in the third and final section, Nietzsche's penchant for stereotyping is brought to the fore, setting the stage for Chap. 4's sustained critique of *Beyond Good and Evil*'s rogues' gallery of 'herd,' 'slave,' and 'rabble' types.

Keywords Nietzsche • *Daybreak* • Morality • Custom • Deck-stacking • Self-contradiction • Ascetics • Stereotypes

© The Author(s), under exclusive license to Springer Nature
Switzerland AG 2023
F. Cauchi, *Nietzsche's Rhetoric*,
https://doi.org/10.1007/978-3-031-42964-4_3

INTRODUCTION

Daybreak contains the seeds and in some cases the full-blown blossom of some of Nietzsche's most famous ideas. These include: Nietzsche's onto-logical/metaphysical principle of 'will to power' (D 18, KSA 3:30–32 and passim); the thinker or free spirit (D 56, KSA 3:57–58 and passim) who "offers himself and his life as a sacrifice" to knowledge (D 459, KSA 3:276); the deleterious effects of pity, most notably the increased suffering for both parties (D 18 and passim); and the purported origin of morality in custom and tradition (D 9, KSA 3:21–24 and passim). However, while the majority of these ideas and insights still stand up to modern-day scru-tiny, the genealogy of morals as set forth in *Daybreak* is more master class in the strategic use of rhetorical devices than solid argument.[1] Repetition, opposition, hyperbole, and the rhetorical question, together with an assortment of logical fallacies such as deck stacking, question begging, sweeping generalization, and false equivalence, will be shown in the first section of this chapter to militate against the genealogy of morals that the text is positing.

Another distinctive feature of *Daybreak*'s rhetorical style (already flagged in Chap. 1) is an incremental and cumulative method of argumen-tation whereby successive aphorisms build up purported evidence in support of a proposition. A typical example of this method[2] can be found in *Daybreak* aphorisms 475–481, in which Nietzsche presents consecutive accounts of the type of hardships to which solitary thinkers like himself willingly subject themselves in their uncompromising pursuit of knowl-edge. The cumulative effect of these sequential experiential accounts is to lend support to the proposition, introduced in the last of the seven-aphorism series, that great thinkers *live* their thoughts. Plato, Spinoza, Pascal, Rousseau, and Goethe—but not Kant and Schopenhauer—have all personally experienced "the vicissitudes and convulsions" of a solitary life that "burns with the passion of thinking." Their thought reflects the pas-

---

[1] In a similar vein, Allison (2001, 80–81) remarks that when we read Nietzsche's views in *The Gay Science* on the subject of ethics and morality, "we are struck by the excess, the hyper-bole, and the evocative force of his pronouncements." But he goes on to affirm that these incitements and provocations on Nietzsche's part are a calculated strategy to address both the heart and the mind of the reader and thereby afford the reader an insight into the cogni-tive and affective resources "through which we come to understand, value, and feel things."

[2] Another example of Nietzsche's cumulative method in *Daybreak* is the opening sections of Book V, i.e., D 423–429 (KSA 3:259–265).

sionate and "involuntary biography" of their soul (D 481, KSA 3:285–286; cf. BGE 6, KSA 5:19–20).[3]

The involuntary biography of Nietzsche's soul is the subject of the second section of this chapter. In a letter to his sister penned shortly after completing *Daybreak*, Nietzsche counsels her to read the book "from an entirely personal point of view ... Seek out everything that you guess is *what* might be useful for your brother and what he might need most, *what* he wants and does not want. In particular you should read the fifth book, where much is written between the lines"[4]—much, yes, but by no means all. The opening aphorism of Book V, for example, requires no reading between lines. On the contrary, it speaks directly to the reader in a hushed, intimate first-person voice that opens a window onto Nietzsche's soul. Gazing upon the early evening silence of the Ligurian Sea (Nietzsche wrote *Daybreak* on the shores of the Italian Riviera) and musing over the human mind's inability to glimpse, let alone penetrate, the hidden mysteries of nature, Nietzsche "begin[s] to hate speech, to hate even thinking; for do I not hear behind every word the laughter of error, of imagination, of the spirit of delusion? Must I not mock at my pity? Mock at my mockery?" (D 423, KSA 3:259–260).

Nietzsche's self-mockery and/or acknowledgment of his own implication in the prejudices and proclivities he is wont to ridicule or revile in others, sometimes takes the form of an internal dialogue; instances of these can be found in Books IV (D 226, 232, 234, 255, KSA 3: 196–208) and V (D 465, 472, 477, 483, 490–494, KSA 3:279–291) of *Daybreak*.

---

[3] As noted in Chap. 1, it is perplexing to find Nietzsche towards the end of the text advising his readers to "dip into" the book rather than read it cover to cover (D 454, KSA 3:274). One (cynical) reason might be his assumption that the reader has already been proceeding sequentially and has therefore been led long enough by the nose to be cut loose for the final furlong. In his 1965 work *Nietzsche as Philosopher*, Danto (1965, 19) takes Nietzsche at his word and goes so far as to claim that "[a]ny given aphorism or essay might as easily have been placed in one volume as in another without much affecting the unity or structure of either"; that not one of Nietzsche's books "presupposes an acquaintance with any other"; and that "his writings may be read in pretty much any order, without this greatly impeding the comprehension of his ideas." The last two assertions are contradicted by Nietzsche himself in his preface to the *Genealogy*: "—If anyone finds this script incomprehensible and hard on the ears, the fault, it seems to me, is not necessarily mine. It [the text] is clear enough, assuming, as I do, that people have first read my earlier works without sparing themselves some effort" (GM Pref. 8, KSA 6:255, opening dash in the original).

[4] This letter, along with others Nietzsche wrote in 1881 and in which he makes specific reference to *Daybreak*, appears in the appendix to Ansell-Pearson and Bamford (2021, 255).

By means of this device, Nietzsche admits to his faults, foibles, moods, and inner conflicts. In doing so, he follows his own advice to the sage who wishes to lead his followers onto the precarious path of knowledge, "there is need from time to of a sign of a conciliatory and gentler humanity: and by that I mean … not only a display of wit and a certain self-mockery, but a self-contradiction" (D 469, KSA 3:281).[5] However, since Nietzsche is only sporadically in full self-disclosure mode, my principal objective in the second section of this chapter is to tease out the self-contradictions that lie hidden within the interstices of text and subtext. In the chapter's last section, I will take a preliminary look at Nietzsche's propensity towards stereotyping—to be more closely examined in Chap. 4.

STACKING THE DECK: MORALITY AS OBEDIENCE TO CUSTOM

Busily at work in the first nine aphorisms of *Daybreak* is the aforesaid cumulative method of argumentation. Nietzsche begins this aphoristic series with a sweeping generalization, followed by two rhetorical questions freighted with two loaded adverbs ('constantly' and 'wantonly'),

> All things that live long are gradually so saturated with reason that their origin in unreason [*Unvernunft*] thereby becomes improbable. Does not almost [*fast*] every precise history of an origination impress our feelings as paradoxical and wantonly offensive? Does the good historian not, at bottom, constantly [*fortwährend*] *contradict*? (D 1, KSA 3:19)[6]

Implicit in the above opening statement is the view that, however improbable it may seem, the origin in unreason of something long deemed reasonable is not only probable but certain. This view is then asserted as fact under the guise of two rhetorical questions, the first of which begs the

---

[5] Cf. "It is part of the humanity of a master to warn his pupil about himself" (D 447, KSA 3:271). See also D 487 & 488, KSA 3:288–289.

[6] Cf. "Almost all the problems of philosophy once again pose the same form of question as they did two thousand years ago: how can something originate in its opposite, for example, rationality [*Vernünftiges*] in irrationality [*Vernunftlosen*], the sentient in the dead, logic in unlogic, disinterested contemplation in covetous desire, living for others in egoism, truth in error?" (HH1, KSA 2:23).

question of a 'precise' genealogy,[7] while the epithet in the second shores up the begged question in the first. In the subsequent eight aphorisms (D 2–9, KSA 3:19–24), the 'precise' historian Nietzsche gives successive examples of mankind's past and present ignorance concerning the 'precise' origin of things. These examples, already previewed in Chap. 1, are as follows: The naïve prejudice of the learned who believe that compared to earlier ages they "*now know better*" what is good and evil, praiseworthy and blameworthy (D 2); the ascription of a moral significance to "all that exists" (D 3—note the predeterminer 'all,' to be discussed below); the imagination's coloring of the world with "*false* grandeur" (D 4); mankind's former fear of gods and its own dreams (D 5); and lastly, belief in appearances (D 6), including imaginary (D 7) and supernatural things (D 8). The eight-aphorism series ends with Nietzsche's "chief proposition" in Book I of the text, namely that morality is merely "obedience to customs" (D 9).

Nietzsche employs the same method at the start of Book II, introducing his chief proposition early on, but only after a series of prefatory aphorisms that provide cumulative anticipatory support by way of example. His chief proposition in Book II, a corollary of the one in Book I, is that "all moral judgment" (note, once again, the predeterminer 'all') is based not on truth but on "*errors*" (D 103, KSA 3:91–92). The lead-up to this proposition (D 97–102, KSA 3:89–91) is as follows. Nietzsche begins in bombastic fashion with the bold, deck-stacking assertion that "[s]ubjection to morality can be slavish or vain or self-interested or resigned or gloomily enthusiastic or an act of despair" (D 97). In other words, what one believes to be a moral act of submission is in fact submission to a particular drive or affect (first error). It is the removal of these "errors," these false beliefs, that fall under the category of what in D 98 is called "*successful crimes*"—Nietzsche's ironic epithet for "innovations in moral thinking." In D 99, we are told that in spite of these innovations, our feelings still drive us to act upon judgments and teachings in which we no longer believe (second error). This is followed in D 100 by an analogy between

---

[7] I concur with May (1999, 73) that Nietzsche's genealogies are fictions. But whereas I see these fictions as tendentious, May sees them as salutary: "a genealogy, even if fictional, simply provides a way of thinking about the present functions and motivations of our ethical concepts, practices, and values by seeing them as contingent successors to possible earlier or more elementary functions and motivations in a manner which is free of the search for timeless 'groundings' ... [and] from the immense authority of tradition and habit by which they are hallowed, so that their value to us may be reassessed in terms of our deepest ethical commitments."

the erroneous ancient belief in "the music of the spheres" and the equally erroneous contemporary belief in "the moral significance of existence" (third error). Dismissing the latter belief as a dream from which we will one day awaken (D 100), Nietzsche ups the rhetorical ante in D 101, first by vilifying as "dishonest, cowardly, lazy!"—strains of 'Truth and Lies' here—those who adopt a belief merely on the basis of custom (fourth error), and second by repeating the provocative predicates in his rhetorical question, "[C]ould dishonesty, cowardice, and laziness be the preconditions of morality?" Lastly, in D 102, the reader is regaled with a burst of thigh-slapping derision aimed at those who judge the moral behavior of others on the basis of their own personal reaction to them (fifth error):

> Threefold error! Threefold primeval blunder! Perhaps inherited from the animals and their power of judgment! Is the *origin of all morality* not to be sought in the detestable petty conclusions: "what harms *me* is something *evil* (harmful in itself); what is useful *to me* is something *good* (beneficent and advantageous in itself); what is useful to me *once or several times* is the inimical in and of itself; what is useful to me *once or several times* is the friendly in and of itself." *O pudenda origo!* (D 102)

The predeterminer 'all,' seen here in the phrase "the origin of all morality," is often used by Nietzsche to anchor what purports to be a claim, but is in fact a sweeping generalization. A particularly risible example of this, i.e., in which the practice of using sweeping generalizations is criticized by means of the same practice, can be found in BGE 198:

> All these morals directed at the individual person to promote what people call his "happiness" ... they are all baroque in form and unreasonable (because they are directed at "everyone," because they generalize what should not be generalized); they all speak unconditionally, consider themselves unconditional. (KSA 3:118)[8]

In D 14 (KSA 3:26–28), entitled 'The significance of madness in the history of morality,' we catch Nietzsche red-handed, generalizing what

---

[8] In his book-length reading of BGE, Lampert (2001) makes a number of references to Nietzsche's broad generalizations, but does not view them as problematic in terms of the claims Nietzsche is making.

should not be generalized and speaking unconditionally.[9] In this aphorism, the predeterminer 'all' appears no less than five times: "all the communities of mankind," "all earlier people," "all ancient mankind," "all superior men," and "almost all the significant men of ancient civilization." A similar rhetorical device is the adverb 'constantly' [*fortwährend*], which in Book I of *Daybreak* is generally used to exaggerate "that terrible pressure, the 'morality of custom,' under which all the communities of mankind have lived" (D 14, KSA 3:). The following aphorisms are exemplary. In D 11 (KSA 3:25), "The morality which prevails in a community" is said to be constantly reinforced by "everybody" through the entrenched habit of linking guilt to punishment. In D 16 (KSA 3:29), a species of custom said to be extant among barbarous peoples and consisting solely of superfluous stipulations is mooted to serve no further purpose than "to keep constantly in mind the constant proximity of custom, the perpetual [*unausgesetzt*] compulsion to practice customs." For neither of these claims does Nietzsche offer any anthropological evidence, relying instead on the cumulative force of repetitive hyperbole. The aphorism is brought to a close with the blanket and presumably facetious statement that the "mighty proposition with which civilization begins" is that "any custom is better than no custom." In D 39 (KSA 3:46–47), the ascetic's periodic moments of ecstasy are diagnosed by Nietzsche as symptomatic of a nervous state of "chronic over-excitability," induced by the body's constant subjection to a punitive regime of "*pure spirituality.*" And in D 77 (KSA 3:74–76) the same "spiritual torture" is said to be one that is constantly preached by Christianity.[10] In short, neither the repetitive hyperbole nor the predeterminer 'all' give credible support to Nietzsche's claim regarding "that terrible pressure, the 'morality of custom,' under which all the communities of mankind have lived."

[9] Nietzsche's work is rife with paradoxes such as the one just cited ("they all speak unconditionally") and cannot, I believe, be indulgently construed as either rhetorical excess or an instance of Nietzsche willfully defying the time-honored practices of traditional Western philosophy. To quote Poellner (2000, 2) on the subject, "it is often pointed out that even if one ignores Nietzsche's provocative and rhetorically overstated paradoxes (e.g., to the effect that all our knowledge is false), there still seem to remain a plethora of contradictions and confusions in his statements on just about any issue." From among this plethora, Poellner extracts some of Nietzsche's most flagrant abuses of logical consistency.

[10] That self-inflicted torture is a touchstone of Christianity is a source of ironic amusement for Nietzsche, who traces the belief that "*voluntary suffering*" is something "meaningful and valuable" back to paganism: "Cruelty is one of the oldest festive joys of mankind. Consequently, people think that the gods too are refreshed and in festive mood when they are offered the spectacle of cruelty" (D 18, KSA 3:30).

Nietzsche's proposition that Christian morality is merely an outgrowth of custom and tradition first appears in *Human*, penned three years before *Daybreak*,

> To be moral, to act in accordance with custom, to be ethical means to prac-tice obedience towards a law or tradition established from of old ... He is called "good" who does what is customary as if by nature ... To be evil is "not to act in accordance with custom," to practice things not sanctioned by custom, to resist tradition, however rational or stupid that tradition may be. (HH 96, KSA 2:92–93)

However, unlike the unvarnished diction of the above passage, the same morality/custom claim is prosecuted in D 9 (KSA 3:21–24) through a dizzying array of rhetorical ploys. Entitled 'Concept of morality of cus-tom' and one of the longest aphorisms in Book I, D 9 begins in *faux* homiletic style, which swiftly modulates into a *faux* apologetic tone. The combined effect of this courteous and conciliatory preamble is to heighten the rhetorical effect of the highly provocative proposition that is about to follow—a provocation that is further heightened by the drum-roll effect of the verb 'slander.'

> In comparison with the mode of life of whole millennia of mankind we present-day men live in a very immoral age: the power of custom is astonish-ingly enfeebled and the moral sense so rarefied and lofty it may be described as having more or less evaporated. That is why the fundamental insights into the origin of morality are so difficult for us latecomers, and even when we have acquired them we find it impossible to enunciate them, because they sound so uncouth or because they seem to slander morality! This is, for example, already the case with the *chief proposition*: morality is nothing other (therefore *no more!*) than obedience to customs, of whatever kind they may be; customs, however, are the *traditional* way of behaving and evalu-ating. (D 9)

Having stated his chief proposition, Nietzsche proceeds to drive it home through the rhetorical staples of repetition, opposition,[11] sweeping generalization, and false equivalence:

---

[11] Opposition plays a key role in classical rhetorical theory and practice. As Goodwin (1999, 92) notes: "Within the canon of *inventio*, for example, we find appeals to the 'advan-tageous' paired with the 'disadvantageous' ... 'guilt' with 'innocence,' 'praise' with 'blame' ... [And] within *memoria* and *actio-pronuntiatio*, we find a spectrum of normative terms marked, at either extreme, by pairs such as 'natural' and 'artificial' ... 'high' and 'low,' and the like."

In things in which no tradition commands, there is no morality; and the less life is determined by tradition, the smaller the circle of morality. The free human being is immoral because in all things he is *determined* to depend upon himself and not upon a tradition: in all the original conditions of mankind, "evil" signifies the same as "individual," "free," "capricious," "unusual," "unforeseen," "incalculable." Judged by the standard of these conditions, if an action is performed *not* because tradition commands it but for other motives (because of its usefulness to the individual, for example), even indeed for precisely the motives which once founded the tradition, it is called immoral and is felt to be so by him who performed it: for it was not performed in obedience to tradition. What is tradition? A higher authority which one obeys, not because it commands what is *useful* to us, but because it *commands*. What distinguishes this feeling in the presence of tradition from the feeling of fear in general? It is fear in the presence of a higher intellect which here commands, of an incomprehensible, indefinite power, of something more than personal—there is *superstition* in this fear. (D 9)

Nietzsche begins the above-quoted segment by reducing his core claim to a simple, mnemonic, slogan-like formula encapsulated in the anaphoric equation: No tradition, no morality—the type of saying that lends itself to the ear rather than to the eye. To quote Nietzsche's Zarathustra, "Whoever writes in blood and proverbs does not want to be read, but to be learned by heart" (Z1 'On Reading and Writing,' KSA 4:48). And in D 9, I would argue, the rhetorical performance wants to be experienced rather than examined. Having delivered his 'no tradition/no morality' proposition, he then rephrases it for no other reason, it would seem, than to keep the declared identity between morality and tradition *constantly* in the mind of the reader. This is followed by the aphorism's key opposition between tradition and "the free human being," which in turn is followed by the predeterminer 'all' in the sweeping statement: "in all the original conditions of mankind, 'evil' signifies the same as 'individual,' 'free,' 'capricious,' 'unusual,' 'unforeseen,' 'incalculable.'" Here, the central antithesis between tradition and freedom is heavily deck-stacked by the excessive use of descriptors for 'free' as compared with the insistent repetition of 'tradition' and 'command.' Lastly, the yoking of tradition and command and of command and fear is demonstrably false. First, as cited earlier in this section, "[s]ubjection to morality can be slavish or vain or self-interested or resigned or gloomily enthusiastic or an act of despair" (D 97). None of these predicates immediately suggest fear. Second, tradition is very often felt by individual members of a community to instill a sense of belonging, security, and identity. It is also a source of pleasure, as Nietzsche points out in *Human,*

An important species of pleasure, and thus an important source of custom, originates in habit. One does what is habitual better and more easily and thus prefers to do it, one derives a sense of pleasure from it and knows from experience that the habitual has proved itself and is thus useful ... one perceives that all customs, even the harshest, grow milder and more pleasant in course of time, and that even the strictest mode of life can become habitual and thus a source of pleasure. (HH 97, KSA 2:94)

In short, Nietzsche's propensity towards sweeping statements and asymmetrical polarities serves less to strengthen his genealogy of morals than to weaken it.

As Babich (2006, 177–178) reminds us, the subtitle to *On the Genealogy of Morals*—Nietzsche's book-length sequel to the *Daybreak* genealogy discussed above—is *A Polemic*. It is indeed. And the strategies Nietzsche deploys in staging this polemic are spelled out for us—unwittingly, perhaps—towards the end of the *Genealogy*'s third essay, where Nietzsche makes passing reference to the "forcing, adjusting, abbreviating, omitting, padding, inventing, falsifying and everything else *essential* to interpretation" (GM III:24, KSA 5:400). He makes a far more direct reference to his rhetorical practice in the *Genealogy* in his retrospective work *Ecce Homo*, "Each time a beginning *meant* to mislead: cool, scientific, even ironic, deliberately foreground, deliberately holding back" (EH 'Genealogy', KSA 6:352). To these two revealing statements I would like to add a third. In the final section of his preface to the *Genealogy* (GM Pref. 8, KSA 5:255–256), Nietzsche holds that "[a]n aphorism, properly stamped and molded, has not been 'deciphered' just because it has been read out; on the contrary, this is just the beginning of its proper *interpretation*, and for this, an art of interpretation is needed."

As I have endeavored to show in the first section of this chapter, the art of interpreting Nietzsche's aphorisms requires a critical eye, ever alert to the rhetorical arts of "forcing, adjusting, abbreviating, omitting, padding, inventing, falsifying and everything else *essential* to interpretation." It also requires an eye for Nietzsche's background art of cumulative argumentation.

SELF-CONTRADICTIONS: MARTYRS, ASCETICS, AND THE VITA CONTEMPLATIVA

If Nietzsche's chief proposition in Book I of *Daybreak* is that morality originated in obedience to custom, his secondary proposition is that mankind's "worst sickness" is the "anaesthetizing and intoxicating" consolations prescribed by Christian "physicians of the soul" (D 52, KSA 3:56). These consolations, he argues, are prescribed as a cure for that other sickness, namely, the belief that life is suffering.[12] "Faith in intoxication," rails Nietzsche, has been preached by a "noble little community of unruly, fantastic, half-crazy people of genius who cannot control themselves" and who see in "everything else" an obstruction to this intoxication. It is a faith, he continues, that has produced an effect "so oppressive, so poisonous to air and land," to have "thoroughly ruined" mankind as a whole (D 50, KSA 3:54–55; cf. D 66, KSA 3:64). What is so striking about this aphorism is not the hyperbolic rhetoric, nor the slippery slope implausibility of an intermittent enjoyment of "moments of ecstasy and exaltation" gradually inducing in mankind a wholesale "contempt for the age and the world," but Nietzsche's own unruly vehemence. This is particularly surprising given Nietzsche's sustained attack in *Human* against the emotional excess and lack of self-control that in his view typifies the pious.[13] To this excess he counterposes a "morality of reason" (WS 45, KSA 2:573–574), oriented towards "self-conquest" [*Selbstbesiegung*] (HH 55, KSA 2:74–75) and a "continual self-restraint [*Selbstbeherrschung*] and self-overcoming [*Selbstüberwindung*] practiced in the greatest and smallest of things" (WS 45)—the type of self-restraint, in fact, that is so often lacking in Nietzsche's rhetoric.

[12] Suffering as the universal constant of human life is a belief that underpins Schopenhauer's philosophy of pity. See his 1850 essay 'On the Suffering of the World' (Schopenhauer, 1970).
[13] The same animus towards the cult of feeling is evident in other passages from Book 1 of *Daybreak*. In four successive aphorisms (D 32–35, KSA 3:41–44), Nietzsche delivers censorious blanket statements on the subject of moral feelings. We are told that one would much rather "suffer for the sake of morality" and thereby feel oneself "*exalted* above reality" than not suffer at all (D 32); that "wherever a man's feelings are *exalted*," even in today's post-Enlightenment world, an "imaginary world is involved in some way" (D 33); that moral feelings precede moral concepts, the former being merely "acquired and well-exercised" inclinations and aversions that one observes and imitates as a child" (D 34); and lastly, that these feelings originate in the judgments and evaluations of our grandparents and that instead of trusting in them we should look "to the gods which are in *us*: our reason and our experience" (D 35).

And yet, despite Nietzsche's call for a morality of reason, and despite his admiration for the Jesuits' ascetic discipline (HH 55), his work contains as many satires and full-scale attacks on asceticism as it does exhortations to the ascetic mode of life. Take the following satire from Book II of *Daybreak*:

> The creation of the world: perhaps it was then thought of by some Indian dreamer as an ascetic operation on the part of a god! Perhaps the god wanted to banish himself into active and moving nature as into an instrument of torture, in order thereby to feel his bliss and power doubled? And supposing it was a god of love: what enjoyment for such a god to create *suffering* men, to suffer divinely and superhumanly from the ceaseless torment of the sight of them, and thus to tyrannize over himself! And even supposing it was not only a god of love, but also a god of holiness and sinlessness: what deliriums of the divine ascetic can be imagined when he creates sin and sinners and eternal damnation and under his heaven and throne a vast abode of eternal affliction and eternal groaning and sighing! (D 113, KSA 3:103–104)[14]

Earlier in the same aphorism, Nietzsche writes of the feeling of "triumph" and "highest enjoyment" experienced by the ascetic when he beholds within himself

> man split asunder into a sufferer and a spectator, and henceforth gazes out into the outer world only in order to gather as it were wood for his own pyre, this final tragedy of the drive for distinction in which there is only one character burning and consuming himself … [producing] an unspeakable happiness at the *sight of torment*! Indeed, happiness, conceived of as the liveliest feeling of power [*Gefühl der Macht*], has perhaps been nowhere greater on earth than in the souls of superstitious ascetics. (D 113, KSA 3:103)

These two passages take on a very different hue, however, when read alongside the astonishingly frank aphorism that immediately succeeds them:

> *On the knowledge acquired through suffering* … The tremendous tension imparted to the intellect by its desire to oppose and counter pain makes him see everything he now beholds in a new light … He thinks with contempt

---

[14] D 113 presages the third essay of Nietzsche's *Genealogy* entitled 'What do Ascetic Ideals Mean?'

of the warm, comfortable misty world in which the healthy man thought-lessly wanders; he thinks with contempt of the noblest and most beloved of the illusions in which he himself formerly indulged; he takes pleasure in conjuring up this contempt as though out of the deepest depths of Hell and thus subjecting his soul to the bitterest pain ... With dreadful clear-sightedness as to the nature of his being, he cries to himself: "For once be your own accuser and executioner, for once take your suffering as the pun-ishment inflicted by yourself upon yourself! Enjoy your superiority as judge; more, enjoy your willful pleasure, your tyrannical arbitrariness! Raise your-self above your life as above your suffering, look down into the deep and the unfathomable depths!" Our pride towers up as never before: it discovers an incomparable stimulus in opposing such a tyrant as pain is. (D 114, KSA 3:104–106)

Suffice to say that the pleasure taken by the invalid in D 114 is *affec-tively* indistinguishable from the "superstitious ascetic" in D 113. While the former not only defies physical pain but intensifies it by chewing heart-ily on the bitterest pill of self-contempt, the latter derives triumphant plea-sure and the liveliest feeling of power in being simultaneously sufferer, spectator, and tormentor. In both cases, the intrinsic link between pleasure and power—a cornerstone of Nietzsche's philosophy—is identical. What differentiates the two is orientation: Whereas the Christian martyr suffers for the greater glory of God, the martyr to knowledge suffers from having "killed" God and thereby "unchained the earth from its sun" (GS 125, KSA 3:480–482; these words belong to Nietzsche's "madman," one of the many masks worn by Nietzsche). Orientation aside, both martyrs experience the same suffering and the same self-inflicted torture as the putatively 'free' spirits who have sought to "*stir up the swamp*" and whose "age-old tragedy" is in Nietzsche's view the only truly important theme of world-history:

Every smallest step in the field of free thought, of a life shaped personally, has always had to be fought for with spiritual and bodily tortures: not only the step forward, no! the step itself, movement, change of any kind has needed its innumerable martyrs through all the long path-seeking and foundation-laying millennia. (D 18, KSA 3:31)

Another parallel between "the so-called religious *nature*" and Nietzsche's madman can be discerned in D 41 (KSA 3:48–49). Just as the religious type has "at all times" (note the predeterminer 'all') sought "to darken the heavens [and] to blot out the sun" for those inclined towards the *vita activa* (cf. D 64, KSA 3:63; D 106, KSA 3:93–94; and D 136, KSA 3:129), so too does Nietzsche's madman. Lantern in hand, he runs into the market square of modernity loudly lamenting the death of God and alerting the jeering bystanders to the darkness of the earth, now that it has been cut loose from the sun: "Who gave us the sponge to wipe away the entire horizon? ... Aren't we straying as though through an infinite nothing? ... Hasn't it got colder? Isn't night and more night coming again and again? Don't lanterns have to be lit in the morning?" (GS 125).

Similar parallels between the Christian ascetic and the solitary thinker can be found in D 440 (KSA 3:269). The latter is said to renounce the world and choose the *vita contemplativa* because to remain in the *vita practica*, given what he knows of his own inclinations, would be "renunciation, melancholy [and] destruction of himself" (cf. D 473, KSA 3:283). But is the same not true of the Christian ascetic? In *Daybreak*, Nietzsche admits to having need of these periods of isolation in order to keep in check the fear and anger that arises within him whenever he finds himself settling into conventional thoughts and habits (D 491, KSA 3:290). However, we learn from his late prefaces to *Human* that the same isolation brought with it the "fears and frosts" of solitude (HH1 P1, KSA 2:13–15), greatly amplified by the "sullen wrathfulness" with which Nietzsche took sides against himself in the years prior to writing *Human* (see HH2 P2 & 4, KSA 2:371–374).[15]

In Book IV of *Daybreak*, Nietzsche frankly acknowledges the likeness, namely, the consonance between the "holy men" who betake themselves to desert, mountain, or pillar to torment themselves to the point of madness and "all superior men who were irresistibly drawn to throw off the yoke of any kind of morality and to frame new laws (D 14, KSA 3:27–28). "We who think differently," he writes in Book IV, "expose ourselves to our own deserts, swamps, and icy mountains, and voluntarily choose pain and self-satiety, as the stylites did" (D 343, KSA 3:237; cf. "Philosophy as I have understood it and lived it so far is a life lived freely in ice and high mountains," EH Pref. 3, KSA 6:258). Committed to "a life shaped personally" (D 18, KSA 3:31), these "superior," solitary men experience their "new passion" for knowledge as a compulsion for which no sacrifice is too great (D 429, KSA 3:264–265). But with sacrifice comes suffering: suffering from self-experimentation (D 501, KSA 3:294), from flesh-lacerating

---

[15]Ackerman (1990, 107) notes that Nietzsche's works repeatedly focus on four 'social positions,' or what I would refer to as 'types': the artist, the philosopher, the scientist and the saint. As I am arguing in this section, the typological features of the philosopher and the saint/ascetic are intrinsically consonant.

truths (D 460, KSA 3:277), and from the malice (D 382, KSA 3:248 and D 522, KSA 3:301), mockery, and laughter of friend or foe (D 41, KSA 3:48–49; D 154, KSA 3:143; and D 484, KSA 3:287)—or in Nietzsche's case, of oneself. Turning the "thumbscrew" of uncompromising honesty against themselves (D 536, KSA 3:306), these martyrs to knowledge subject themselves to the ascetic discipline of metaphorical fasting and abstinence (D 14, KSA 3:26–28), denying themselves the warmth and comfort of long-cherished illusions.

The most explicit account of the identity between the two ascetic types is given by Nietzsche in the third essay ('What do Ascetic Ideals Mean?') of his *Genealogy*,

These nay-sayers and outsiders of today, those who are absolute in one thing, their demand for intellectual cleanliness, these hard, strict, abstinent, heroic spirits who make up the glory of our time, all these pale atheists, Antichrists, immoralists, nihilists, these sceptics, ephectics, *hectics* of the spirit (they are one and all [*hectics* of the spirit], in a certain sense), these last idealists of knowledge in whom, alone, intellectual conscience dwells and is embodied these days,—they believe they are all as liberated as possible from the ascetic ideal, these "free, *very* free spirits": and yet, I will tell them what they themselves cannot see—because they are standing too close to themselves—this ideal is quite simply *their* ideal as well, they themselves represent it nowadays, and perhaps no one else, they themselves are its most intellectualized product ... its most insidious, delicate and elusive form of seduction:—if I am at all able to solve riddles, I wish to claim to do so with *this* pronouncement! ... These are very far from being *free* spirits: *because they still believe in truth* ... (GM III:24, KSA 6:398-399, ellipses in the original)

Note Nietzsche's reference to the "hard, strict, abstinent" qualities of these nay-sayers and, more tellingly, the ruthless thumbscrew-honesty of his implicit self-identification with "all these pale atheists," whose *hectic* spirit is consonant with the "mad" medieval Christian saints pilloried by Nietzsche in D 14.[16]

---

[16] As Janaway (2007, 173) notes, from Section 10 to the end of the third essay of the *Genealogy*, the figure of the ascetic priest is "often entwined with that of the philosopher." It is also worth remembering Clark's (1990, 168) warning that the third essay's initial distinction between philosophers and ascetic priests is "deliberately misleading." It is indeed. In GM III:10 (KSA 5:360), Nietzsche describes the "peculiarly withdrawn attitude of the philosophers, denying the world, hostile to life, suspicious of the senses, [and] freed from sensuality" as a necessary "disguise and cocoon," an "ascetic mask" without which the philosophic spirit would not have been possible at all. But in GM III:24 (KSA 5:398–401), that mask is stripped away.

In short, trying to discriminate between the ascetic and the genuine free spirit is so much time lost. Both live in figurative deserts and mountains—Nietzsche's shorthand for a reclusive, contemplative solitude that brings knowledge and danger in equal measure—and both sacrifice themselves to a higher ideal. One of the most affecting accounts of this danger is given by Zarathustra's shadow, who recounts to his master (another mountain dweller) the sufferings and hardships they have jointly endured on account of Zarathustra's uncompromising pursuit of knowledge:

> "With you I have haunted the remotest, coldest worlds …
> With you I strove to enter everything forbidden …
> With you I smashed whatever my heart revered …
> With you I unlearned my faith in words and values and great names …
> What did I have left? A heart weary and insolent; a restless will; fluttering wings; a broken backbone.
> Ever a visitor, searching for *my* home, oh Zarathustra … it devours me.
> 'Where is—*my* home?' I asked, and I search and searched for it, but I have not found it. Oh eternal everywhere, oh eternal nowhere, oh eternal—in vain!"
> Thus spoke the shadow, and Zarathustra's face lengthened at these words. "You are my shadow!" he said at last, with sadness. (Z4 'The Shadow,' KSA 4:339-341)

An earlier incarnation of Zarathustra's shadow is the titular 'wanderer' in *The Wanderer and his Shadow* (the title of Part 2, Volume II of *Human*). Here, the 'wanderer' is Nietzsche's epithet for the free spirit and knowledge seeker who, like Zarathustra's shadow, is destined to roam without destination because life itself—the life he seeks to watch and observe—is transient and ever-changing. Fraught with danger, the journey will take him into deserts on which the sun "burn[s] like a god of wrath" and "dreadful night" descends when the heart of the wanderer grows weary of wandering (HH 638, KSA 2:362--363). To reiterate, trying to differentiate between a stylite and a seeker after truth is time lost.

STEREOTYPES

One of the more disturbing features of Nietzsche's rhetoric and the central focus of Chap. 4 of this study is its invidious propensity towards stereotyping. Book IV of *Daybreak* contains two egregious examples, the first of which is his dual speculation that the cause of black skin pigmentation might be "the ultimate effect of frequent attacks of rage (and undercurrents of blood beneath the skin) accumulated over thousands of years," and that the white skin of the *"more intelligent* races" is the effect of "an equally frequent terror and growing pallor" (D 241, KSA 3:202). The second example is the claim, not hypothesis, that those of mixed racial descent are marked by "a disharmony of physical features," in parallel to which one "must always find a disharmony of habits and value-concepts" (D 272, KSA 3:213)—a preposterous inference and one that Nietzsche also makes in his discussion of Socrates in *Twilight* (to be critiqued at length in Chap. 5). In D 272, Nietzsche attempts to shore up his 'mixed race' claim with a parenthetic and doubtless apocryphal reference to "(Livingstone [who] heard someone say: 'God created white and black men but the Devil created the half-breeds')" (ibid.). That Nietzsche drags in science (the "undercurrents of blood") to support his first hypothesis (D 241) and gives the appearance of disowning the quip quoted in the second (D 272) by placing it in parentheses, merely adds insult to injury. Marginally less invidious stereotyping relates to the Jewish people, "the best haters there have ever been," who paradoxically "invented" the commandment "Love your enemies!" (D 377, KSA 3:246). He makes the same claim about the Christians, for whom he fashions the epithet "great haters" (D 411, KSA 3:254–255).

Less offensive instances of stereotyping in *Daybreak* relate to Nietzsche's diagnosis of revenge, or what he would later refer to as '*ressentiment*,' as the dominant drive in Christian 'types.'[17] In the first essay of his *Genealogy*, Nietzsche uses this French noun to denote the underlying impulse of the "slave revolt" in morality. According to this theory, "*ressentiment* itself turns creative and gives birth to values" when those who are denied the "proper response of action" to a felt slight, compensate with "imaginary

---

[17] May (1999, 42–43) identifies three principal features which distinguish *ressentiment* from resentment: "first, its object of hatred is universal in scope, embracing, at the limit, all of existence; second, it thoroughly falsifies that object in order to render the latter inescapably blameworthy—which, at the limit, means that it falsifies the whole character of existence; and, third, since such universal resentment is impossible to satisfy, its revenge must be, at least in part, imaginary." *Ressentiment* blame is universal, explains May, because "the slave's rage is directed at the suffering which, in and of its very nature, existence generates."

revenge."[18] In *Daybreak*, we encounter a number of 'types' whose revenge places them within the 'slave morality' mindset. One of these is the mystic type, to which the holy man (discussed in the previous section) belongs. These men consider their true self to manifest itself in moments of anaesthetizing "exaltation and ecstasy." Accordingly, they harbor vengeful feelings towards "their environment, their age, their entire world" to which they erroneously attribute their wretched condition, but which Nietzsche roots in their neurasthenia (D 50, KSA 3:54–55, cf. D 39, KSA 3:46–47, quoted in the previous section). But see the long passage from GM III 24 (also quoted in the previous section), in which Nietzsche categorizes all the "nay-sayers and outsiders of today"—i.e., those who challenge the contemporary mores, values, and assumptions—as, on the one hand, the "heroic spirits who make up the glory of our time," and, on the other, as "*hectics* of the spirit."[19]

We meet the same 'type' of hectic-heroic spirits in D 18 (KSA 3:30), in the type of soul that takes pleasure in the cruelty of voluntary suffering and is said to be strong, vengeful, hostile, sly, and suspicious, "ready for the most fearful things and made hard by deprivation and morality."[20] It is the same voluntary suffering of self-deprivation which, as Nietzsche confesses, threatens to reduce ruthlessly honest free spirits like himself to become "virtuous monsters and scarecrows," were it not for their recourse to the exuberant arts (GS 107; KSA 3:463–465)—the sort of arts on poignant display in the caricature and self-parody of Part 4 of *Zarathustra*. We encounter the same self-deprivation in Nietzsche's late prefaces to *Human* (written shortly after *Zarathustra* Part 4), in which he recalls the

---

[18] In glossing the concept of *ressentiment*, Deleuze (1983, 111) emphasizes that *ressentiment* must not be defined in terms of "the strength of a reaction." This is because the man of *ressentiment* does *not* re-act: "the word *ressentiment* gives a definite clue: *reaction ceases to be acted in order to become something felt* (*senti*). Reactive forces prevail over active forces because they escape their action." For other readings of Nietzsche's *ressentiment*, see Scheler (1961) and Bittner (1994).

[19] As a philologist, Nietzsche would have been aware that the German word '*hektiker*' has its etymological roots in the Greek *hektikos*, which the ancient Greek physicians used to refer to a feverish condition. www.etymonline.com/word/hectic.

[20] It is, I suspect, passages such as these which inform Solomon's (1994, 105) masterful unmasking of the contradictions and self-contradictions inherent in Nietzsche's vilification of the feeling of *ressentiment*. "There is no emotion [i.e. *ressentiment*]," writes Solomon "more clever, more powerful, more life-preserving, if not life 'enhancing,' no emotion more conducive to the grand act of revenge that Nietzsche himself wishes to perpetrate on modernity and the Christian world."

eviscerating suffering of ascetic self-denial or *"disciplina voluntatis"* to which he had voluntarily subjected himself in the six-year hiatus between *The Birth of Tragedy* and the writing of *Human* (HH2 P1-2, KSA 2:369–372). It was during this period that he inflicted upon himself a brutal regimen of solitude, skepticism and self-administered "anti-Romanticism," the ghosts of which, i.e., Schopenhauer and Wagner, come back to haunt him in Part 4 of *Zarathustra* in the respective guises of the Soothsayer and the Sorcerer.[21]

Nietzsche's reassessment (and self-purging) of Wagner furnishes the template for another stereotype in *Daybreak*, namely, the artist. In D 41 (KSA 3:48–49), Nietzsche uses an extremely broad brush to delineate artists as generally "unbearable, capricious, envious, violent." But the envy and violence with which Nietzsche tars the generic artist has its roots in his own increasingly (self-)critical stance towards Wagner ("I was even one of the most corrupted Wagnerians," CW 3, KSA 6:16). This stance is elaborated upon in Nietzsche's 1888 essays *The Case of Wagner* and *Nietzsche Contra Wagner*, but it was in 1878, three years before *Daybreak*, that Nietzsche specifically attributed envy and violence to Wagner:

> [Wagner] is not sure of himself, but distrustful and arrogant. His *art* has this effect upon artists, it is envious of all rivals. (KSA 8: NF 1878, 27[54]:496)

> All Wagner's ideas straightaway become manias; he is *tyrannized* over by them ... For instance, by his hatred of Jews. He *kills* his themes like his "ideas," by means of his violent love of repeating them. (KSA 8: NF 1878, 27[90]:502)

As Scheier (1994, 451) reminds us, Wagner represented for Nietzsche "the contemporary paradigm of *the* artist"—not, of course, the Wagner of *The Birth of Tragedy*, whom Nietzsche envisaged as accomplishing through his mythopoeic operas the rebirth of Dionysian tragedy out of the spirit of music.[22]

---

[21] For an extended reading of these and the other "higher men" who track Zarathustra down in his mountain retreat, see Cauchi (2018).

[22] "*The Birth of Tragedy*," continues Scheier (1994, 452), "had proclaimed as the *task* of Bayreuth: that the tragedian Wagner and the philosopher Nietzsche together would revoke the fateful error of the philosopher Socrates and tragedian Euripides—namely, the introduction of logical optimism into the history of European mankind (BT 18)."

It is important, however, to balance Nietzsche's negative stereotyping with his positive stereotyping. I shall limit myself to three, selected with a view to providing a salutary counterweight to Nietzsche's customary stance towards Jews and Christians. The first is a paean to the people of Israel. In D 205 (KSA 3:181), Nietzsche writes of their "extraordinary" psychological and spiritual resources, learned from the rich history of their forefathers, whose "coldest self-possession and endurance in fearful situations ... their courage beneath the cloak of miserable submission, their heroism in *spernere se sperni*, surpasses the virtues of all the saints." The second positive stereotype is Nietzsche's highly romanticized depiction of the Catholic priesthood. In D 60 (KSA 3:60–61), he writes of "an inborn grace of gesture, the eye of command, and beautiful hands and feet," especially in priests of noble descent. He also reads in their face the attainment of "that total spiritualization," which in Nietzsche's view is the felicitous effect of a priestly mode of life, typified by a successful taming of the beast within. The negative version of this priestly type of "total spiritualization" is given in D 331 (KSA 3:234), in which asceticism is declared to be "the right discipline for those who have to exterminate their sensual drives because the latter are raging beasts of prey. But only for those!" The same positive–negative polarity can be found in my third example, Blaise Pascal. In D 64 (KSA 3:63), Nietzsche mocks Pascal for having "attempted the experiment of seeing whether, with the aid of the most incisive knowledge, everyone could be brought to despair: the experiment miscarried." And a few aphorisms later, mining the same satirical vein, Nietzsche declares that "[w]hatever proceeds from the stomach, the intestines, the beating of the heart, the nerves, the bile, the semen—all those distempers, debilitations, excitations, the whole chance operation of the machine of which we still know so little!—had to be seen by a Christian such as Pascal as a moral and religious phenomenon" (D 86, KSA 3:80–81). Offsetting these good-humored satirical gibes, however, is Nietzsche's warm and sincere portrayal of Pascal as the incarnation of the Christian ideal, who "in unity of fervor, spirit, and honesty [was] the first of all Christians" (D 192, KSA 3:165).[23]

---

[23] In a recent online essay, Parr confidently affirms that "Nietzsche loved Pascal." In support of his claim, Parr cites numerous (more than a hundred) *Nachlass* passages in which Nietzsche refers to Pascal. "In his final books," continues Parr, "Nietzsche attacked Pascal with the complex ferocity and passion of a lover."

In 1888, the year before madness engulfed him, Nietzsche reflects (albeit selectively) upon the book he had written seven years earlier. There is, he writes, "not a single negative word in the entire book [*Daybreak*], not a single attack or piece of malice … instead, it lies in the sun, round and happy like a sea creature sunning itself between rocks" (EH 'Daybreak' 1, KSA 3:329). This lack of malice, or what Nietzsche calls "the sunshine and gentleness of grace" (D 449, KSA 3:272) or "a conciliatory and gentler humanity" (D 469, KSA 3:281), is at its most visible in his earnest desire not only to avoid the infliction of suffering on others (see, for example, D 457, KSA 3:275–276 & D 512, KSA 3:298), but also to give succor to "the needy in spirit … to *give away* one's spiritual house and possessions, like a father confessor who sits in his corner anxious for *one in need* to come and articulate the distress of his mind, so that he may again fill his hands and his heart and *make light* his troubled soul!" (D 449, KSA 3:271–272). And as Nietzsche reminds us shortly before the end of *Daybreak*, the solitary thinker must himself practice respect, for "[i]f we are not as considerate of the honor of other people in our private soliloquies as we are in public, we are not behaving decently" (D 569, KSA 3:330 cf. D 528, KSA 3:303).

If, however, despite his best intentions, Nietzsche is not always as conciliatory and gracious in *Daybreak* as he might have been, he is rarely so in the book he wrote five years later. As we shall see in the next chapter, the Nietzsche who in *Daybreak* suns himself lizard-like on Genoan rocks, has in *Beyond Good and Evil* mutated into a northern hemisphere leviathan. In place of the playful satire of the former text, a work to which not even "the slightest whiff of gunpowder" is said to cling (EH 'Daybreak' 1, KSA 6:329), weapons-grade malice bursts through the rhetorical fabric of *Beyond Good and Evil*.

References

Ackerman, Robert John. 1990. *Nietzsche: A Frenzied Look*. Amherst: The University of Massachusetts Press.

Allison, David B. 2001. *Reading the New Nietzsche: The Birth of Tragedy, The Gay Science, Thus Spoke Zarathustra, and On the Genealogy of Morals*. Lanham: Rowman & Littlefield.

Ansell-Pearson, Keith, and Rebecca Bamford. 2021. *Nietzsche's Daybreak: Philosophy, Ethics, and the Passion of Knowledge*. Oxford: Wiley-Blackwell.

Babich, Babette E. 2006. The *Genealogy of Morals* and right reading: On the Nietzschean aphorism and the art of the polemic. In *Nietzsche's 'On the Genealogy of Morals': Critical Essays*, ed. Christa Davis Acampora, 177–190. Lanham: Rowman & Littlefield.

Bittner, Rüdiger. 1994. *Ressentiment*. In *Nietzsche, Genealogy, Morality*, ed. Richard Schacht, 127–136. Berkeley: University of California Press.

Cauchi, Francesca. 2018. *Zarathustra Contra Zarathustra: The Tragic Buffoon.* London: Routledge.

Clark, Maudemarie. 1990. *Nietzsche on Truth and Philosophy.* New York: Cambridge University Press.

Danto, Arthur C. 1965. *Nietzsche as Philosopher.* New York: Macmillan.

Deleuze, Gilles. 1983. *Nietzsche and Philosophy.* Trans. Hugh Tomlinson. New York: Columbia University Press. Original edition: 1962. *Nietzsche et la philosophie.* Paris: Presses universitaires de France.

Goodwin, David. 1999. Toward a grammar and rhetoric of visual opposition. *Rhetoric Review* 18 (1): 92–111.

Janaway, Christopher. 2007. *Beyond Selflessness: Reading Nietzsche's 'Genealogy.'* New York: Oxford University Press.

Lampert, Laurence. 2001. *Nietzsche's Task: An Interpretation of 'Beyond Good and Evil.'* New Haven and London: Yale University Press.

May, Simon. 1999. *Nietzsche's Ethics and his War on 'Morality.'* New York: Oxford University Press.

Nietzsche, Friedrich. 2007a. *Human, All Too Human: A Book for Free Spirits.* Trans. R. J. Hollingdale. Cambridge: Cambridge University Press.

———. 2006a. *Daybreak: Thoughts on the Prejudices of Morality.* Trans. R. J. Hollingdale. Cambridge: Cambridge University Press.

———. 2001a. *The Gay Science.* Trans. Josefine Nauckhoff. New York: Cambridge University Press.

———. 2001b. *Thus Spoke Zarathustra: A Book for All and None.* Trans. Adrian Del Caro. New York: Cambridge University Press.

———. 2002. *Beyond Good and Evil: Prelude to a Philosophy of the Future.* Trans. Judith Norman. Cambridge: Cambridge University Press.

———. 2007b. *On the Genealogy of Morality.* Trans. Carol Diethe. New York: Cambridge University Press.

———. 2006b. *The Anti-Christ, Ecce Homo, Twilight of the Idols, and Other Writings.* Trans. Judith Norman. New York: Cambridge University Press.

Parr, Jamie. n.d. The alchemy of suffering: Blaise Pascal and the transformation of despair into love. https://www.abc.net.au/religion/how-to-read-blaise-pascal-pensees/11540800.

Poellner, Peter. 2000. *Nietzsche and Metaphysics.* New York: Oxford University Press.

Scheier, Claus-Artur. 1994. The rationale of Nietzsche's *Genealogy of Morals*. In *Nietzsche, Genealogy, Morality*, ed. Richard Schacht, 449–459. Berkeley: University of California Press.

Scheler, Max. 1961. *Ressentiment*. Trans. William W. Holdheim. New York: Free Press of Glencoe.

Schopenhauer, Arthur. 1970. *Essays and Aphorisms*. Trans. R. J. Hollingdale. London: Penguin.

Solomon, Robert C. 1994. One hundred years of *ressentiment*: Nietzsche's *Genealogy of Morals*. In *Nietzsche, Genealogy, Morality*, ed. Richard Schacht, 95–126. Berkeley: University of California Press.

CHAPTER 4

Rank, Types, and Pejorative Epithets

Beyond Good and Evil: Prelude to a Philosophy of the Future (1886)

Abstract The twofold aim of this chapter is as follows: On the one hand, it seeks to challenge the 'perspectivist' approach to Nietzsche's work by confronting *Beyond Good and Evil*'s core postulate of an "unalterable, inborn order of rank [*Rangordnung*]" (BGE 263, KSA 5:263). And on the other hand, it seeks to expose the equally unalterable "spiritual *fatum*" of deep-seated prejudices (BGE 231, KSA 5:170) underpinning that postulate and to which (i.e., both the prejudices and the postulate) Nietzsche accords epistemic privilege. The noun '*Rangordnung*' appears more times—seventeen, to be precise—in *Beyond Good and Evil* than it does in any of Nietzsche's other published works. It occurs several times in both volumes of *Human, All Too Human*. But whereas in the latter text it denotes a "spiritual order of rank" (AOM 362, KSA 2:523), or an "order of rank of desirable things [*der Güter*] and of morality" (HH 42, KSA 2:65), in the former it denotes something innate and therefore fixed. The chapter is divided into three sections, each of which illuminates the particular rhetorical strategies deployed by Nietzsche to affirm and adduce his *Rangordnung* claim. The first section provides a detailed exposition and critique of the text's adjectival epithets 'common,' 'herd,' and 'slave,' together with their corresponding compound nouns such as 'herd-men,' 'herd-instinct,' and 'herd-morality,' whereby Nietzsche classifies and essentializes 'ignoble' ranks and types. The second section draws attention to the text's ambiguous use of the word 'blood' and of the verb '*züchten*,'

© The Author(s), under exclusive license to Springer Nature Switzerland AG 2023
F. Cauchi, *Nietzsche's Rhetoric*,
https://doi.org/10.1007/978-3-031-42964-4_4

meaning to breed, grow, or cultivate. The final section highlights the text's emphatically unambiguous use of the adjectives 'fundamental,' 'natural,' 'instinctive,' and 'degenerate.'

Keywords Nietzsche • *Beyond Good and Evil* • Rank • Types • Common • Herd • Slave • Breeding • Lineage • Essentializing

INTRODUCTION

Any commentator seeking to uphold Nietzsche's perspectivism—the view that there are no facts, only interpretations (KSA 12: NF 1878, 7[60]:315)[1]—would be hard pressed when confronted with "the unalterable, inborn order of rank" (BGE 263, KSA 5:217) advanced in *Beyond Good and Evil* (hereafter 'BGE' or 'the text'). At first blush, the text's early allusions to bias, its ubiquitous references to taste [*Geschmack*], Nietzsche's oft-expressed disgust with ideas and temperaments other than his own, and his avowed "assumption" towards the end of the text that his readers have been fully aware from the outset that the truths expressed in the work are "*my* truths" (BGE 231, KSA 5:170), all furnish ample grist for the perspectivist camp's mill. At odds with this reading, however, is the text's rigid classification of 'noble' and 'ignoble'

---

[1]The "flamboyant relativism" of this famous line, writes Solomon (1996, 196-197), has typically been misinterpreted, "first, by leaping to the unwarranted conclusion that interpretation therefore has no basis and perspectives cannot be compared; and second, by similarly leaping to the conclusion that perspectivism leaves no grounds for evaluation. In its most vulgar form: 'one interpretation is as good as any other.'" But, continues Solomon, the *ad hominem* approach to philosophy that typifies Nietzsche's philosophical practice evaluates an interpretation on the basis of the person who generates it. For example, "If it is a claim about justice, is it that of virtuous Socrates or of brutish Thrasymachus?" The position I am taking in this monograph is that Nietzsche is substantially invested in his interpretations, many of which he presents as truths or as corrections of entrenched philosophical errors. Indeed, as Nehamas (1985, 35 & 40) astutely points out, the difficulty (I would be more inclined to call it a contradiction) at the heart of Nietzsche's writing is that on the one hand, he wants his readers to accept his views, judgments, and values, and on the other, he wants them to understand that these are *his* views, judgments, and values. "He is constantly resisting the dogmatic self-effacement [which for Nietzsche is endemic in all philosophical discourse] that is directed at convincing an audience that the views with which they are presented are not their authors' creations but simply reflections of the way things are." That is why, concludes Nehamas, Nietzsche deploys many styles, i.e., to deflect attention from "his single project to present an interpretation that demands to be believed even as it says that it is only an interpretation."

types and the "inborn [*eingeboren*] order of rank" to which each type is said to belong on the basis of their inherited traits. As noted in Chap. 1, BGE contains seventeen iterations of the word *Rangordnung* [order of rank].

These traits are given in BGE as follows. The noble type (of soul) is strong, independent, and predestined for command, whereas the ignoble type is obedient, tormented, and "half-bestial" in the impoverishment of its soul (BGE 61, KSA 5:80). The noble type is dominant, authoritative, and self-sufficient, whereas the ignoble is dependent, useful, and mediocre (BGE 206, KSA 5:133-134). The noble soul is acutely aware of the chasm separating "man and man" (BGE 62, KSA 5:83), whereas the ignoble soul seeks equality and the "green pasture happiness of the herd" (BGE 44, KSA 5:61). The noble soul is able to withstand profound suffering—indeed, order of rank is held by Nietzsche to be "almost determined by just *how* deeply people can suffer" (BGE 270, KSA 5:225), whereas the ignoble soul seeks safety, security, and contentment (BGE 44, KSA 5:61). The noble soul possesses an instinct for cleanliness (BGE 271, KSA 5:226–227), compared with the stench that reportedly clings to the ignoble soul (BGE 30, KSA 5:49). Lastly, a noble life characterized by *otium* (BGE 204, KSA 5:130) and *lento* (BGE 256, KSA 5:203) is distinct from the busy life of the "useful, industrious, abundantly serviceable, and able herd animal man" type (BGE 242, KSA 5:183).

This stereotyping, or what Leiter (2014, 6) refers to as a "Doctrine of Types," presupposes that "[e]ach person has a fixed psycho-physical constitution, which defines him as a particular *type* of person." It also presupposes that this fixed constitution will determine a type's tastes and value judgments. In BGE, Nietzsche's tastes and value judgments are writ large in the vivid and visceral adjectival epithets and compound nouns with which he depicts the 'ignoble' types and their constitutive psycho-physical traits. These distinctive lexical features will be enumerated and discussed in the second section of this chapter. In the chapter's third and fourth sections, I shall examine two other lexical features of the text which similarly exhibit a propensity to essentialize types: first, the ambiguous use of the word 'blood' and of the verb '*züchten*,' meaning to breed, grow, or cultivate; and second, the text's unambiguous use of the adjectives 'degenerate,' 'fundamental,' 'natural,' and 'instinctive.' These latter, I shall argue, read far more like dogmatic pronouncements on the intrinsic nature of the 'ignoble' type than expressions of the author's personal taste.

Despite Nietzsche's trumpeting of taste, his words all too often betray the epistemic privilege he accords his own psycho-physical or affective-evaluative responses. A conspicuous example of this is the epistemic privilege he grants to "*our* truths" (BGE 202, KSA 5:124) and "obvious truths" (BGE 229, KSA 5:165)—truths for which there are allegedly no ears because people are too fearful to acknowledge them—but not to truths "best suited to mediocre minds" (BGE 253, KSA 5:196), or to philosophers' truths, which he scare quotes and dismisses as disguised prejudices (BGE 5, KSA 5:19). Indeed, Nietzsche's use of scare quotes is arguably the most prominent marker of epistemic privilege in his work and one that is all-pervasive in BGE. Another example of epistemic privilege in the text is the confident assertion that the "*pathos of distance,*" which for Nietzsche epitomizes the noble type, "grows out of the ingrained differences between stations." Without this type of pathos, he proclaims, "the enhancement of the type 'man,' the constant 'self-overcoming of man' (to use a moral formula in a supra-moral sense)" would not be possible (BGE 257, KSA 5:205).

'This dissonance' in the text between its perspectival pretensions and its dogmatic pronouncements raises the theoretical question of the relationship between taste and truth claims—a question that in recent years has preoccupied Nietzsche commentators. I shall begin with a brief account of the current debate.

Taste, Affects, and Epistemic Privilege

There is broad scholarly consensus that Nietzsche equates judgments of taste with value judgments and that these value judgments are grounded in the affects. What has recently been debated, however, is whether these affective-evaluative states are akin to Humean sentiments and thus make no objective claim as to how the world really is (anti-realism),[2] or whether Nietzsche deems his own evaluative judgments and those of like-minded individuals to have epistemic privilege over rival evaluative judgments. Standing on either side of the debate is Leiter (2014) and Mitchell (2017). Leiter (2014, 120) adduces as evidence of Nietzsche's anti-realist position—i.e., there are no objective facts about value—Nietzsche's

---

[2] In Book III of *A Treatise of Human Nature*, Hume (1960, 457–458) asserts that moral judgments are not derived from reason, which "is perfectly inert," but instead are moral sentiments or feelings which in turn express affective states. "Since morals ... have an influence on the actions and affections, it follows, that they cannot be deriv'd from reason; and that because reason alone, as we have already prov'd, can never have any such influence. Morals excite passions, and produce or prevent actions. Reason of itself is utterly impotent in this particular. The rules of morality, therefore, are not conclusions of our reason."

"relentless pursuit of the psycho-physiological roots of our value judgments" as well as the following statement from *The Gay Science*: "Whatever has *value* in our world now does not have value in itself, according to its nature—nature is always valueless, but has been given value at some time" (GS 301, KSA 540; cf. D 3, KSA 3:19–20). Mitchell (2017, 43), on the other hand, cites the following passage from the *On the Genealogy of Morals* as "the strongest textual evidence" that, contra Humean sentiment qua subjective preference, Nietzsche considers our pre-reflective affective response to things to be a more reliable source of knowledge than rational demonstrations and proofs: "the *more* affects we are able to put into words about a thing ... the more complete will be our 'concept' of the thing, our 'objectivity'" (GM III:12, KSA 5:365). Mitchell's scare quotes alert the reader to Nietzsche's epistemological skepticism—i.e., the ineluctably human perspective of all our knowledge—which grounds his 1873 essay 'On Truth and Lies in a Nonmoral Sense' (see Chap. 2 of this study). The opposing positions expressed in the *Gay Science* and *Genealogy* citations above are, I believe, a case of Nietzsche revising his earlier opinion—a prerogative that in his view attests to an individual's integrity, intellectual growth, and lack of personal vanity (see HH 527 & 637[3]).

As noted above, BGE furnishes ample evidence in support of Mitchell's contention that Nietzsche accords epistemic privilege to his own affective-evaluative responses. In this respect, it is important to bear in mind that the knowledge afforded by these responses is not restricted to self-knowledge, but extends to objects, people, and actions. As Poellner (2000, 232) points out, our affective response to an object, person, or action is experienced as "not merely contingently *caused*, but as *merited* by the object's intrinsic character."[4] One such object for Nietzsche is the Bible. In BGE 52 (KSA 5:72), he states that a person's taste for the Old Testament

---

[3] "One person retains an opinion because he flatters himself it was his own discovery, another because he acquired it with effort and is proud of having grasped it: thus both do so out of vanity" (HH 527, KSA 2:325). "Redeemed from the fire [of the passions], driven now by the spirit, we advance from opinion to opinion ... as noble *traitors* to all things that can in any way be betrayed—and yet we feel no sense of guilt" (HH 637, KSA 2: 362).

[4] In a recent article, Drapela (2020, 86) defends the anti-realist reading of Nietzsche, arguing that Nietzsche "does not view judgments of taste as responding to objective evaluative features of objects, nor does he believe that his evaluative judgments have any special status such that others ought to make the same judgments." While I agree with Drapela that Nietzsche does not think others should make the same judgments, I believe that the reason for this is the epistemic privilege Nietzsche accords his own superior evaluative judgments and, by extension, the incomprehensibility of such judgments to those of inferior taste and judgment.

is a "touchstone" for the greatness of their soul, whereas a preference for the New Testament, "the book of mercy," attests to its smallness. Another of Nietzsche's examples is the so-called truths of philosophers. Philosophers who believe that things assigned the highest value cannot possibly originate in "taste and inclination" and the affective chaos of feelings, but rather in God or the 'thing in itself,' are "fools—at best." This way of judging [*urtheilen*], he adds, "typifies the prejudices" [*Vorurtheilen*] by which metaphysicians of all ages can be recognized (BGE 2, KSA 5:16–17). To which I would add that this rhetorical mode of argumentation, already discussed in Chap. 2, typifies one of the ways in which Nietzsche exploits etymology to bolster his claims.[5] In this particular instance, the contiguous repetition of the root word '*urtheil*' serves to reinforce Nietzsche's contention that judgment [*Urtheil*] is rooted in prejudice [*Vorurtheil*]—a contention which in this chapter will be specifically applied to Nietzsche's categorization of 'herd,' 'rabble,' and 'slave' types.

Having thus established that for Nietzsche taste is an infallible index of a person's affective manifold and concomitant prejudices, the question that now needs to be asked is what Nietzsche's taste/evaluative judgments tell us about the nature of his own affective manifold. Conway's (1994, 182) answer is as trenchant today as it was thirty years ago, namely that Nietzsche's valorization of the 'noble'—or, to be more precise, of what he designates as the characteristic qualities of the 'noble' individual—is symptomatic of an underlying decadence. Nietzsche's writings, contends Conway, irrespective of whether they were written early or late in his career, "are rife with signs of his decadence: lapses into romanticism and resentment, delusions of grandeur, irrational appeals to race and power, fantasies of virile heroes and chivalrous warriors, an unquenchable thirst for revenge and redemption, an anachronistic reverence for 'noble' ideas, and so on." Writing in the same year as Conway, Solomon (1994, 106) asks, "Why should the 'poison' [*ressentiment*] that fuelled [Nietzsche's] genius be the source of such (self-?) contempt for him? How did Nietzsche think himself to be escaping the vicious psychological circle involved in

---

[5] An early example of this occurs in BGE 11 (KSA 5:25), in which Nietzsche plays on the words '*finden*' [find] and '*erfinden*' [invent] to mock German Romantic philosophy for its confounding of imagination and intuition (see also BGE 12, KSA 5:26–27). Another favorite pun of Nietzsche's is '*Versuch*' [attempt or experiment] and '*Versuchung*' [temptation], which he invariably uses to typify the courage and audacity of his imaginary "philosophers of the future" (see, for example, BGE 42, KSA 5:59 & BGE 205, KSA 5:133).

resenting his own resentment—a dubious form of 'self-overcoming' or 'undergoing' in any case?"

The poison in Nietzsche's own affective manifold is the focus of the remainder of this chapter. A meticulous examination of BGE's rhetorical formations through which Nietzsche essentializes types out of particular patterns of affective-evaluative responses; ranks these types as either noble or ignoble; and vilifies the latter, will disclose the deep-seated prejudices driving Nietzsche's own affective-evaluative responses. To cite, once again, the following lines from *Daybreak*: "Whenever a person reveals something, one can ask: What is it supposed to conceal? From what is it supposed to divert the eyes? What prejudice is it supposed to arouse? And additionally: How far does the subtlety of this dissimulation go? And in what way has it failed?" (D 523, KSA 3:301). Accordingly, if Nietzsche's distinction between noble and slave is an attempt "to revitalize a decadent and decaying society with a Hellenic vision" (Ackerman, 1990, 107), it is an attempt that is mired in the very decadence and *ressentiment* diagnosed by Nietzsche (see Conway and Solomon above) and implicit in the epithets scrutinized below. The successive punches of these reiterated epithets, I would argue, effect a gradual stupefaction of the reader's critical faculties—a brick wall of critical numbness that fails to register the "brick wall of spiritual *fatum*" underlying Nietzsche's affective-evaluative responses. It is this failure which the following three sections seek to rectify by breaching the wall of mind-numbing epithets and exposing the prejudices that underwrite them.

UNPACKING THE PUNCH OF NIETZSCHE'S EPITHETS

Nietzsche's preferred epithets in the text for the ignoble type are 'common,' 'rabble,' 'herd,' and 'slave.' A representative profile of this type can be found in Part 2 of *Zarathustra*. In a discourse entitled 'On the Rabble [*Gesindel*],' the reader is exposed to a vitriolic deluge of quite breathtaking force, even allowing for the fact that it is delivered through the mouth of its fictional protagonist. In this discourse, Zarathustra fulminates over the rabble's "grinning snouts" and "dirty dreams," which have "poisoned" the well of life and driven the non-rabble type into the wilderness, where they would rather die of thirst than share the well of life with "filthy camel drivers." "Are poisoned wells and stinking fires and soiled dreams and maggots required in life's bread?" asks Zarathustra—note here Nietzsche's parodic, biblical use of polysyndeton, e.g., "And Adam gave names to all cattle, and to the fowl of the air, and to every beast of the field" (Gen. 2.20). It is a rhetorical question of course, the contemplation of which he finds even more nauseating than the knowledge that life itself necessitates enmity and death (KSA 4:124–125). In BGE, the rabble type is presented to the reader as a compound noun, *Pöbel-Typus*, a word-formation strategy that arguably reifies the 'rabble-type' into a distinct species. This reification is heightened by the corresponding compound nouns 'rabble-man' [*Pöbelmann*] and 'rabble-instinct' [*pöbelmännische Instinkt*]. Nietzsche uses the same compound noun device in his depiction of both 'herd' and 'slave' types (to be discussed in sequence below) and uses the epithet 'common' [*gemein*] to denote the defining quality of all three kindred types, i.e., rabble, herd, and slave.

Common

The first thing to note about the German adjective *'gemein'* is that it carries considerably more negative freight than its English equivalent 'common.'[6] The reason for this is etymological.[7] The English word 'common' is derived from the Middle English, Anglo-French *commun*, which in turn is derived from the Latin cognate *communis*, meaning communal or held in common (as in a plot of land). The German adjective *'gemein,'* however, derives from Old High German *gimeini*, cognate with Old English *gemǣne*, meaning mean. *Gemein* comprises three distinct but far from mutually exclusive meanings: small-minded and petty (mean); a lack of some essential high quality of mind or spirit (ignoble); and degradation, debasement, or servility (abject) (Merriam-Webster). Langenscheidt lists

---

[6] In her translation of BGE for Cambridge University Press, Judith Norman (see Nietzsche, 2002, 163) chooses to translate *'gemein'* as 'base' rather than 'common' throughout the text in order to bring out the term's derogatory connotations.

[7] In his excellent reading of Nietzsche's theory of 'the slave revolt in morality', Migotti (2006, 118) draws attention to the systematic ambiguities of words like 'noble' and 'common,' single words which "yoke together, on the one hand a politico-genealogical conception of superiority with a meritocratic, characterological one, and on the other hand, an innocuous concept of being shared with a pejorative term of opprobrium." These ambiguities, argues Migotti, cannot be dismissed as simple vagaries of the English language, given that they occur in other European languages such as German (*'vornehm'* and *'gemein'*) and French (*'noble'* and *'commun'*). On the contrary, they reflect two semantic strata: an older one that embodies an aristocratic scheme of value and a younger one that evinces "an accelerating tendency to identify the truly moral with a distinctively impartial, egalitarian mode of evaluation."

mean, nasty, and rotten as the first meaning of *gemein*; vulgar, low, coarse, dirty, and filthy as the second; and common, general, public as the third. Oxford-Duden likewise gives first and second place to the meanings given in Langenscheidt, but inverts the order: coarse and vulgar are given first, followed by nasty, mean, and base. In BGE, all three meanings are at play, either explicitly or implicitly, and not infrequently in the same aphorism.

Of the three meanings of *gemein*, 'common' or 'general' is the easiest to pin down. In BGE 253, for example, Nietzsche yokes together the rhyming *kleine* and *gemeine* to encapsulate the "mediocre minds" of the "mediocre Englishmen—I mean Darwin, John Stuart Mill, and Herbert Spencer," who jointly and severally display a remarkable facility for gathering "lots of common little [*kleine-gemeine*] facts" (BGE 253, KSA 5:196–197). And in BGE 43 (KSA 5:50), Nietzsche writes disdainfully of the 'common good' [*Gemeingut*], portraying it as a contradiction in terms: "whatever can be common [*was gemein sein kann*] will never have much value. In the end, it has to be as it is and has always been: great things are left for the great, abysses for the profound, delicacy and trembling for the subtle, and, all in all, everything rare for those who are rare themselves." Notwithstanding the quotation's nebulous adjectives, Nietzsche's meaning is abundantly clear: What is common can *ipso facto* never be great, profound, subtle, or rare. By proceeding synonymously, Nietzsche gives the impression of advancing a tautological argument: Great things belong to the great (rogue strains of Descartes' ontological argument, here) and abysses to the profound. But it is only *in abstracto* that great and small, abyss and surface are opposed. In living contexts, the opposition is wont to break down, e.g., the profound vacuity of the numbskull, or the smallest deed producing the greatest effect. Of the five adjectives (common, great, profound, subtle, and rare), only 'common' and 'rare' are mutually exclusive; the rest require context.

A similar prejudice against that which is held or shared in common is evident in Nietzsche's withering attacks on Jeremy Bentham's utilitarian conceptualization of the common good. In BGE 228 (KSA 5:163–165), the English utilitarians are variously described as dull, tedious, and soporific, and collectively spurned as "clumsy, conscience-stricken herd animals" who fail to understand that "'general utility,'" "'general welfare,'" or "'the happiness of the majority'" can never be an end or an ideal. They merely signify "an English happiness," encompassing comfort, fashion, and—for the select few—"a seat in Parliament." What is right and just for one, contends Nietzsche, cannot possibly be right and just for another, on account of the "inborn order of rank" that in his view necessarily prevails between people. He launches a similar attack in BGE 190 (KSA 5:111), observing that the origin of every utilitarian morality is the erroneous assumption that what is 'good' is identical with what is "useful and pleasant," which in turn is akin to what Nietzsche scorns as the equally erroneous Socratic assumption that no man would wittingly do himself harm. Both assumptions, we are told, "stink of the *rabble*," the same stench that offends Zarathustra's nostrils and fills him with nausea and disgust at the thought of having to share the well of life with "filthy camel drivers" (Z2 'On the Rabble,' KSA 4:124–125).

The stench [*übelriechend*] of the rabble is a recurring theme in BGE. In BGE 26, Nietzsche declares that the single most noisome task in the life of every philosopher is having to rub shoulders with the hoi polloi. However, if one is to plumb the depths of "herd animal man," asserts Nietzsche, mob-mingling is an inescapable, if loathsome, necessity. That is why he advises the genuine knowledge-seeker to take full advantage of the voluble cynic should chance happen to throw one in one's path. These "base souls" [*gemeine Seele*], we are told, readily recognize within themselves "the animal, the commonplace [*Gemeinheit*], the 'norm.'" They can even be found wallowing in books "as if in their own excrement [*Mist*]" (BGE 26, KSA 5:43–45)—the same books, presumably, as those which, four aphorisms later, are said to be as foul-smelling as the general public for whom they were written. Their "petty-people-stench" [*Kleine-Leute-Geruch*]—note the type-establishing compound noun—permeates the places where the people [*das Volk*] eat and drink, "even where they worship" (BGE 30, KSA 5:48–49). Nevertheless, as Nietzsche concedes much later in the text, *das Volk* have at least been inculcated with respect for the Bible and for similar works bearing the seal of great destiny (cf. AOM 98, KSA 2:417 quoted in Chap. 1):

> It is a great achievement when the masses (the flat and fast intestines of all kinds) have finally had the feeling bred into them that they cannot touch everything, that there are holy experiences which require them to take off their shoes and keep their dirty hands away—and this is pretty much as high a level of humanity as they will ever reach. (BGE 263, KSA 5:218)

Of particular significance here is the gratuitous scatological reference (cf. BGE 26 above) and the emphasis, once again, on the coarse, dirty, filthy meaning of '*gemein*.' Nietzsche goes on to compare the people's learned respect for great works with the "disgusting" and "shameless" way in which the impudent eyes and hands of the "so-called scholars, the devout believers in 'modern ideas' … touch, taste, and feel everything" (BGE 263, KSA 5:218). It is no coincidence, of course, that the vivid images of people wallowing in excrement and leaving their stench on everything with which they come into contact instantly evokes herd-like images in the mind of the reader.

Herd

Nietzsche's pejorative adjectival epithet 'herd' [*Heerde*], together with his visceral contempt for the 'modern ideas' of equality and the common good, is an implicit subversion of the Christian trope of flock and shepherd. He gleefully acknowledges how offensive it must be to many ears when, without euphemism or simile, "someone classifies human beings as animals" and repeatedly uses "expressions like 'herd' and 'herd instincts' with reference to the people of 'modern ideas'" (BGE 202, KSA 5:124).[8] Nevertheless, as Nietzsche *faux*-apologetically explains, "[w]e can't help it, since this is where our new insights happen to lie" (BGE 202, KSA 5:124). These insights, however, give rise to such disgust and repulsion in Nietzsche as to require an entirely new taxonomy capable of capturing the herd-like quality of these human-animal types. This taxonomy largely consists of compound nouns, the densest concentration of which occurs in BGE 199–203 (KSA 5:119–128). In these aphorisms, we read that "herd men" [*Heerdenmenschen*] are driven by "herd instincts" [*Heerden-Instinkte*], chief amongst which is "herd-timidity" [*Heerden-Furchtsamkeit*]. Herd-timidity gives rise to a "herd-mindset" [*Heerden-Denkweise*], which embraces the notion of "herd-utility" [*Heerden-Nützlichkeit*] and conforms to a "herd-morality" [*Heerden-Moral*]. And herd-morality instils a "herd-conscience" [*Heerdengewissen*] and "herd-animal-longings" [*Heerdenthier-Begierden*], both of which are manifest in "herd-maxims" [*Heerden-Maximen*]. It is important to note here that not one of these compound nouns is scare quoted in the text. The reason for this,

---

[8] Hargis (2010, 476) points out that the "nihilistic/engulfing herd" of Nietzsche's post-*Zarathustra* works is vastly different to the "democratic/inclusive herd" of his middle works. Within the latter, argues Hargis, membership in the democratic herd "fosters humility and respect, rendering not only greater equality but also heightened insight and understanding into alternative perspectives and ideas."

I submit, is the epistemic privilege Nietzsche accords his own value judgments.

Another characteristic of the herd type is its "democratic taste," which infuses the "herd-maxims" of equal rights and sympathy for all that suffers. The ultimate goal of these maxims, scoffs Nietzsche, is the abolition of suffering and "the universal, green pasture happiness of the herd, with security, safety, contentment, and an easier life for all" (BGE 44, KSA 5:61)—a parodic riff on the Benthamite concept of the common good. But what is particularly interesting here is that the BGE 44 reference to the democratic taste and the 'modern ideas' that enshrine it echoes the text's earlier reference to "the democratic instincts [*demokratischen Instinkten*] of the modern soul!"—instincts that in Nietzsche's view are driven by "the plebeian antagonism towards all privilege and autocracy" (BGE 22, KSA 5:37). If we set these last two citations side by side, the inference to be drawn is that the democratic taste of the modern soul is rooted in a so-called democratic instinct that is, by its very nature, opposed to "privilege and autocracy." This is consonant with Nietzsche's value theory outlined earlier in the chapter (see 'Taste, Affects, and Epistemic Privilege'), namely that a person's taste is a reflection and thus a reliable index of his or her affective manifold.

In a much later aphorism, however, the causal relation between the democratic instinct and modern ideas is inverted. The "idiotic guilelessness and credulity of 'modern ideas,'" warns Nietzsche, will eventually lead to the "*total degeneration* [*Gesammt-Entartung*] of human beings ... into the perfect herd animal ... into stunted little animals with equal rights and equal claims" (BGE 203, KSA 5:127–128).[9] He makes a similar argument in 'On the Natural History of Morals,' one of the nine titled parts into which the book is divided. The term 'natural history' is illuminating here. It has two primary meanings: (1) a treatise on some aspect of nature, e.g., Hume's *A Treatise of Human Nature*, and (2) the natural development of something (such as an organism or disease) over a period of time

[9] In a footnote to his brief discussion on Nietzsche's organic metaphors, Gemes (1992, 62) gives the following warning: "Those who take seriously the Nietzschean slogan 'a thing is the sum of its effects' will concur with Derrida's (1984, 31) observation that 'There is nothing absolutely contingent about the fact that the only political regimen to have *effectively* brandished his name as a major and official banner was Nazi.' In fact I believe the real question of Nietzsche's culpability is best addressed in terms of his responsibility for fostering a set of metaphors, in particular and most dangerously, the metaphor of degeneration. Nietzsche's complicity rests not in what he said but in his very language itself."

(Merriam-Webster). Only the second meaning is operative in 'On the Natural History of Morals.' In BGE 199, for example, Nietzsche creates the compound epithet "people-herds" or "herd-people" [*Menschenheerden*] to denote "racial groups, communities, tribes, folk, states, [and] churches." Corralled within these communities, "humanity has been the best and longest-standing breeding [*züchten*] ground for the cultivation of obedience." From this *faux*-sociological observation, Nietzsche considers it reasonable to suppose that "the average person has an innate [*angeboren*] need to obey" and that this innate need takes the form of "a type of *formal conscience* that commands ... 'Thou shalt'" (BGE 199, KSA 5:119–120).

The words 'obedience,' 'innate,' and 'formal conscience' (a striking anticipation of Freud's superego), constitute a triadic causal pattern similar to the one highlighted in Chap. 2. Collectively, the three terms shed light on the kind of natural history Nietzsche has in mind in his genealogical account of the democratic taste. To clarify, what Nietzsche is claiming in BGE 199 is that in an environment where obedience prevails, the majority of organisms—in this case, human beings—will naturally develop obedience as their dominant behavioral trait, which in turn will gradually harden into instinct and thus become innate. Before continuing my reading of BGE 199, it will be helpful to clarify what Nietzsche means by 'instinct.' In a notebook fragment from 1881, he writes, "I speak of *instinct* when some judgment (taste at its lowest level) is incorporated [*einverleiben*] so that it now spontaneously stirs itself and need no longer wait for stimuli" (KSA 9: NF 1881, 11[164]:505). As glossed by Constâncio (2011, 93), this ingrained, incorporated, spontaneous, and habitual behavior "functions without mediation, especially without the mediation of consciousness."[10]

At this juncture in BGE 199, Nietzsche shifts into reverse gear, moving from the influence of the environment on natural behaviour to the influence of hereditary traits. The shift comes with the word '*vererbt*,' meaning

---

[10] Constâncio (2011, 93–94) goes on to mention Lupo's (2006) attempt "to distinguish 'instinct' [*Instinkt*] from 'drive' [*Treib*] by claiming that instincts are built on the drives. Judgment and memory, asserts Lupo, consolidate successful responses of the drives to events in the external world, thereby giving rise to *habits*, i.e., well-practiced automatisms, more or less permanent forms of organization and connected activity of the drives. Such (organic) habits are the 'instincts.'" But as Constâncio wisely cautions, Nietzsche often uses the two terms, i.e., instinct and drive, interchangeably, using the word 'drive' "to describe complex and habitual urges (like the 'drive for knowledge') and never explicitly opposes basic drives to (complex) instincts."

inherited or hereditary: "The oddly limited character of human develop-ment—its hesitancy and lengthening, its frequent regressions and rever-sals—is due to the fact that the herd instinct of obedience is inherited the best and at the cost of the art of commanding." The end result, declares Nietzsche, are the "European herd animals" of the late nineteenth cen-tury, whose hereditary obedience has produced tame and useful members of society whose herd values of diligence, moderation, public spirit, good-will, and compassion testify to the "regressions and reversals" of human development (BGE 199, KSA 5:119–120).[11]

It is necessary to pause here, to compare Nietzsche's BGE 199 stance towards obedience with the one he takes in BGE 188 (KSA 5:108–109):

> What is essential and invaluable about every morality is that it is a long com-pulsion ... that there be *obedience* in one direction for a long time. In the long term, this always brings and has brought about something that makes life on earth worth living—for instance: virtue, art, music, dance, reason, intellect—something that transfigures, something refined, fantastic, and divine ... the discipline that thinkers imposed on themselves, thinking within certain guidelines imposed by the church or court or Aristotelian presup-positions, the long, spiritual will to interpret every event according to a Christian scheme ... all this violence, arbitrariness, harshness, terror, and anti-reason has shown itself to be the means through which strength, reck-less curiosity, and subtle agility have been bred into the European spirit. Admittedly, this also entailed an irreplaceable loss of force and spirit, which have had to be crushed, stifled, and ruined ...

The comparison is revealing, for whereas in BGE 199 obedience is said to be an innate attribute of the herd on account of "the herd instinct of obe-dience [being] inherited the best," the same inherited trait is celebrated in BGE 188 as "essential and invaluable," not only for the discipline required

[11] In a similar vein, Nietzsche reviles the Christian precepts of "equality before God" and compassion for "all the sick and suffering" as an "almost willful degeneration and atrophying [*Entartung und Verkümmerung*] of humanity," the end result of which can be seen all over modern-day Europe in the ubiquitous "herd-animal" [*Heerdenthier*] man. Neither strong or far-sighted enough to allow the natural law of "ruin and failure" to run its course, nor noble enough to recognize the "abysmally different orders of rank and chasms in rank between man and man," Christian proselytizers, declares Nietzsche, have been permitted to prevail over the fate of Europe, "until a stunted, almost ridiculous type, a herd animal, something well-meaning, sickly, and mediocre has finally been bred: the European of today ..." (BGE 62, KSA 81–83, ellipsis in the original).

for works of art and the analytical mind, but also for having bred supple-
ness, strength, and audacity into "the European spirit."

Setting aside BGE 188, a core tenet of Nietzsche's natural history of
morals is that hereditary herd values produce useful and obedient members of society. The breeding of "herd utility" (BGE 201, KSA 5:121),
asserts Nietzsche, has propagated and preserved the myriad "failures and
degenerates ... the diseased and infirm." In doing so, it has simultaneously
culled the strong, the virile, the conquering, and the domineering—
instincts which in Nietzsche's classification of types epitomize "the highest
and best-turned-out of the type 'human'" (BGE 62, KSA 5:81–83). In
BGE 201 (KSA 5:121–123), Nietzsche maintains that while the cultivation of herd utility preserves the community and ensures its survival, the
same inbred obedience and utility causes human degeneration and atro-
phy. Drives such as enterprise, daring, cunning, and rapaciousness, which
in more warrior-like epochs were likewise cultivated for the purposes of
common utility (e.g., the defense of the community against marauding
invaders), have in our more peaceable times been forced underground.
Thus, whenever these more dangerous drives periodically erupt, bursting
through the ramparts of 'herd conscience' and striking fear into the 'herd'
members of the community, society denounces them as evil. As a result,
qualities that were once honored as the most trusted servants of the common good, are now emasculated by the 'herd instinct' and its "imperative
of herd timidity: 'We want the day to come when there is *nothing more to
fear!*'"—an imperative, quips Nietzsche, that is currently to be found
strutting across Europe in the guise of 'progress.'

Slave

In BGE 225 (KSA 5:160), Nietzsche makes contemptuous reference to
the "dejected, rebellious slave strata [*Sklaven-Schichten*] which strives for
dominance—they call it 'freedom'" (note, once again, the compound
noun). However, it is not Spartacus and his fellow gladiators whom
Nietzsche has in mind here. Rather, it is the Jacobins of the French
Revolution, an episode in history that Nietzsche refers to as "the last great
slave revolt [*Sklaven-Aufstand*]" (BGE 46, KSA 5:67). The key word here
is the scare quoted 'freedom,' which in BGE is generally aligned with
'herd instinct,' 'democratic instinct,' and 'democratic taste.' It is also used
as an ironic synonym for the modern notion of progress (BGE 260, KSA
5:210). To return to the 'slave' epithet, Nietzsche provides one of his

clearest and fullest expositions of this word in BGE 260. It is in this aphorism, one of the longest in the text, that we first encounter Nietzsche's
concept of 'slave morality,' a concept upon which he would enlarge the
following year in the first essay of his *Genealogy*.[12]

In BGE 260 (KSA 5:208–212), "slave morality" [*Sklaven-Moral*] is juxtaposed to "master morality" [*Herren-Moral*], both compound nouns and
both said to express the values and qualities of those who devised these distinct types of morality.[13] In determining the concept 'good,' the master or
ruling type identifies it with the proud, elevated states of soul which it hon-
ors in itself and views as a determinant of order of rank. The concept 'bad,'
on the other hand, pertains to those natures [*Wesen*] in which the opposite
of such proud, elevated states inhere and whom the ruling type despises.
These creatures are the "slaves and dependents" of all kinds and degrees over
which the dominating type rules. Accordingly, continues Nietzsche, the contrast between 'good' and 'bad' in the master morality is roughly equivalent
to the contrast between 'noble' and 'contemptible'—a contrast noticeably
adopted by Nietzsche throughout the text. These despised beings are characterized as "cowardly, apprehensive, and petty, people who [think] narrowly in terms of utility" and are driven by "the desire for *freedom*, the
instinct for happiness." Accordingly, it is not to be wondered at if the moral
valuations of those who are "violated, oppressed, suffering, unfree, exhausted,
and unsure of themselves" set a premium on qualities that will serve to allevi-
ate their suffering, i.e., pity, patience, industriousness, and humility. In short,
concludes Nietzsche, "slave-morality is essentially a morality of utility," and
wherever the latter type of morality holds sway, the words 'good' and 'stupid' become ever harder to distinguish.

BGE divides the slave type into two main categories: the religious and
the secular. The principal characteristic of the first is said to be a desire for
revenge, while that of the second is a desire for equality and the common
good. There is, however, considerable overlap between the two. I shall
deal with the secular first. Lumped under this head are the following types:

---

[12] The first iteration of the compound noun 'slave morality' [*Sklaven-Moral*] was in a notebook entry written two years earlier, in the spring of 1884. Written in verse form and under
the title 'Causes of Pessimism' are the following lines: "slave morality in the foreground
'equality'/the meanest people have all 'advantages' for themselves/the degeneration of the
rulers and ruling classes/the consequences of the priests and world calumniators/the com-
passionate and sensitive: absence of hardness/... the poor dry spirits, cowardly too" (KSA
11: NF 1884: 25[345]:103).
[13] For a clear and incisive exposition of Nietzsche's 'master' and 'slave' categories, see May
(1999, 41–52).

The "eloquent and prolifically scribbling slaves of the democratic taste and its 'modern ideas,'" who believe themselves to be free spirits but are in fact "a very narrow, restricted, chained-up type of spirit" (BGE 44, KSA 5:60–61); the industrious democrats, whose industriousness is of a piece with that of the scribbling and "presumptuous little dwarf and rabble-man [*Pöbelmann*]" scholar types (BGE 58, KSA 5:77); the socialists; the ideologists of revolution; and even the "anarchist dogs" [*Anarchisten-Hunde*] who appear to be opposed to all of the foregoing, yet harbor the same desire for a "'free society'" (BGE 202, KSA 5:125). As crudely delineated (the straw man fallacy) by Nietzsche (BGE 202, KSA 5:124–126), this free society will be free of any special claims, rights or privileges, on the assumption that a society in which everyone is equal would obviate the need for any so-called rights. Such a society, holds Nietzsche, is neither free nor equitable since those who champion it are driven by an "instinctive hostility towards all forms of society besides that of the *autonomous* herd"—note the deliberate oxymoron here. Note, too, Nietzsche's own instinctive hostility towards all forms of society that manifest "faith in the morality of *communal* pity ... faith in the community as *Redeemer*, which is to say: in the herd, in 'themselves' [*an 'sich'*]." Here, the adjectives 'communal' and 'herd' affirm their synonymous status in BGE, while the Kantian '*an sich*' suggests that the 'thing in itself' of the herd is the herd instinct.

As noted above, the religious slave types are grouped together on the basis of their purportedly shared desire for revenge. The text's first mention of revenge is in connection with Christ's crucifixion, that "hideous superlative" and paradoxical formula "'God on the Cross,'" which Nietzsche counters with his own formula: the crucified Christ versus the values of antiquity. Cast in these world-historical terms, Christ's calvaric sacrifice for the redemption of mankind is seen by Nietzsche not as a vicarious sacrifice for all but rather as the "sacrifice of all freedom, all pride, and all self-confidence of the spirit" (BGE 46, KSA 5:66–67). With Christianity's bold inversion of values, whereby pride was demonized and pity, humility, and self-abasement were valorized, the "slave revolt" in morality was born (BGE 195, KSA 5:116–117). "This was the revenge of the Orient, the *deep* Orient," avers Nietzsche; "this was the revenge of the oriental slave on Rome with its noble and frivolous tolerance." Note the emphasis on 'deep,' evoking a heart-of-darkness type Orientalist trope. Nietzsche continues:

> Slaves want the unconditional; they understand only tyranny, even in moral-
> ity. They love as they hate, without nuance, into the depths, to the point of
> pain and sickness—their copious, *hidden* suffering makes them furious at the
> noble taste that seems to *deny* suffering. (BGE 46, KSA 5:67)

This is a highly instructive passage. To shore up his slave revenge argument, Nietzsche asserts that because tyranny is the only thing that slaves
understand, they will "want" the same tyranny in their morality. This is a
non sequitur, which only holds true if one grants the slave revenge premise. More striking still, and an illustration of my 'instinctive hostility' comment above, is that the fury, hatred, and lack of nuance that Nietzsche
attributes to the slave is arguably manifest in the tenor of the aphorism as
a whole. This lack of nuance is necessitated by the rhetorical objective of
the block quotation, which is to root the alleged unconditional tyranny of
slave morality in the equally unconditional tyranny of a "copious, *hidden*
suffering." Meanwhile, the complementary phrases "into the depths" and
"*hidden* suffering" jointly recuperate the earlier reference to "the *deep*
Orient" in a bid to enhance the suggestion of some kind of smoldering
heart-of-darkness fury.

The slave's desire for revenge is also attributed by Nietzsche to the
industrious, 'rabble-type' scholars, who are said to harbor resentment
towards their philosopher-masters. A mere whiff of "the *otium* [leisure]
and noble opulence of the philosopher's psychic economy," we are told, is
enough to remind "the specialists and pigeon-hole dwellers" of their intellectual limitations (BGE 204, KSA 5:130). In a similar vein, these scientific laborers, who have successfully liberated themselves from the shackles
of theology, now want to "play at being 'master'" by dismissing philosophy as nothing more than "a series of *refuted* systems and wasteful expen-
diture" (BGE 204, KSA 5:129–130). Industrious and insecure (like "all
dependent men and herd animals"), these scholar types possess an "instinct
for mediocrity that instinctively works towards the annihilation of the
exceptional man" (BGE 206, KSA 5:134, cf. BGE 218 & 220, KSA
5:153–155). Once again, Nietzsche's instinctive hostility is on full display
in the hyperbolic noun 'annihilation' and in his insistence that the scholar's desire for revenge is instinctive. In BGE 58, Nietzsche goes so far as
to assert that the ancient lineage of idleness, which he favorably equates
with nobility, is "passed down through the bloodline" (to be discussed in
the next section of this chapter). It would thus account for "the aristocratic feeling that work *defiles* [*schänden*]," which is to say it makes the soul

and the body into something base [*gemein*]."[14] Nietzsche then juxtaposes this noble idleness with the "self-satisfied, stupidly proud industriousness" of modern-day Europe (BGE 58, KSA 5:75–76), herding, yet again, the epithets 'base,' 'dirty,' 'stupid,' and 'industrious' into the field of green pasture contentment.

Revenge is also detected by Nietzsche in the saintly type or what he terms the *homines religiosi* (BGE 45, KSA 5:65). In *Daybreak*, Nietzsche had typified this type as desert-, mountain-, cave-, or pillar-dwelling ascetics, whose defining characteristics are fasting, sexual abstinence, and an all-consuming desire for spiritual ecstasy (D 14, KSA 3:26–28). The same "dietary" regimen is adverted to in BGE 47 (KSA 5:67–69). But whereas in D 14 the rhetorical register is one of gentle ridicule: "Ah, give me madness, you heavenly powers! Madness, that I may at last believe in myself! Give me deliriums and convulsions, sudden lights and darkness," it acquires a far sharper edge in BGE 51 (KSA 5:71). In the latter aphorism, the distressed ascetic souls of D 14 are depicted as monstrosities of negation, negating both the world and—through starvation and celibacy—their own nature. In BGE 59 (KSA 5:78), the Christian ascetic's deified image of an after-life is equated with the philosophers' and artists' "passionate and exaggerated worship of 'pure forms,'" both portrayed by Nietzsche as a prolonged revenge against earthly life. Nevertheless, the extremes to which the saintly ascetics are willing and able to go in denying their bodily needs evinces for Nietzsche a formidable "'will to power'" (BGE 51, KSA 5:71), a tyrannical discipline of the spirit which, like the behavioral trait of obedience discussed in the previous section, is deemed to be necessary for the breeding of a higher spirituality. Indeed, as I argue in my previous monograph (Cauchi 2022), the doctrine of self-overcoming that Nietzsche ventriloquizes through Zarathustra is a fundamentally ascetic practice that bears all the hallmarks of a moral tyranny. So, too, does the "anti-Romantic self-treatment" (see Chap. 3) that Nietzsche inflicted upon himself in the years between the writing of *The Birth of Tragedy* and *Human, All Too Human*, which can also be adduced as a form of self-directed revenge. See Solomon's (1994, 106) comment on Nietzsche's *ressentiment* cited in Chap. 3.

---

[14] Cf. "A higher culture can come into existence only where there are two different castes in society: that of the workers and that of the idle, of those capable of true leisure" (HH 439, KSA 2:286).

As was the case in *Daybreak* (see Chap. 3), there is a great deal of resemblance in BGE between Nietzsche's portrait of the *homines religiosi* and that of the genuine free spirit. The solitude, self-directed cruelty, and high pain threshold of both types mark them out as noble: "Profound suffering makes you noble; it separates" (BGE 270, KSA 225). And just how deeply the knowledge seeker must suffer is made explicit by Nietzsche in his warning to "you philosophers and friends of knowledge"—including himself—to "beware of martyrdom! Of suffering 'for the sake of truth!'" (BGE 25, KSA 5:42). And yet, in a much later aphorism, shorn of the ironic, self-distancing exclamation marks, the line between martyrdom and solitary knowledge seeking is all but erased. The "dangerous thrill of *self*-directed cruelty," purportedly experienced by the ascetic in "puritanical penitential spasms, vivisections of conscience, or a Pascalian *sacrifizio dell'intelletto*," is said to be equally felt by "the knower" [*der Erkennende*] when he forces his spirit "to know *against* its own inclination and, often enough, against the wishes of his heart." Even the act of getting to the bottom of something, adds Nietzsche, is a violation, a desire to hurt "the fundamental will [*Grundwillen*] of the spirit" (BGE 229, KSA 5:165–167). He makes the same comparison in two successive aphorisms towards the end of the text: First, in his reference to "the spiritual, silent arrogance of the sufferer, this pride of knowledge's chosen one, its 'initiate,' almost its martyr" (BGE 270, KA 5:225); and second, in "the strangest and most dangerous solitude," which he associates with the saint and equates with the "highest instinct of cleanliness" (BGE 271, KSA 5:226).

BREEDING AND BIRTHRIGHT

Implicit in the above discussed adjectival epithets and their corresponding compound nouns is an essentializing of what Nietzsche classifies as the 'ignoble' type—an essentialization that is further suggested by the German verb '*züchten*,' meaning to breed, grow, or cultivate. Many of the text's iterations of this verb and its noun form '*Züchtung*' are figurative rather than literal. Take the following '*Zucht/Züchtung und*' formulations: The genuine philosopher, for whom "the overall development of humanity" weighs on his conscience as a personal responsibility, will know how to make use of religion for his work of "breeding and education" [*Züchtungs- und Erziehungswerke*] (BGE 61, KA 5:79), just as the "tyranny" of Asian astrology in the past and the Christian-moral interpretation of human behaviour in the present plays a vital role in "the spirit's discipline and breeding" [*der geistigen Zucht und Züchtung*] (BGE 188, KA 108–110). The sole task of this new kind of genuine philosopher—the kind exemplified by Nietzsche himself—is to prepare the ground for the "breeding and cultivating" [*Zucht und Züchtung*] of humanity by "compel[ling] the will of millennia into *new* channels" and thereby supplanting such utilitarian "nonsense" as the greatest good for the greatest number (BGE 203, KSA 5:126). This new kind of philosopher will demand both of himself and others "critical discipline and every habit [*Zucht und jede Gewöhnung*] that leads to cleanliness and rigor in matters of the spirit" (BGE 210, KSA 5:143). For without this "protracted discipline and practice [*lange Zucht und Übung*] ... [in] the spiritualization of justice and benevolent severity," we can never hope to achieve a higher type of spirituality (BGE 219, KSA 5:154).

In contrast to the spiritual connotation of the verb '*züchten*' outlined above, there are at least five BGE aphorisms in which *züchten* is directly linked either to race or to order of rank. The first of these aphorisms is BGE 200 (KSA 120–121), which opens with the following statement: "In an age of disintegration where the races are mixed together, a person will have the legacy of multiple lineages in his body, which means conflicting (and often not merely conflicting) drives and value standards."[15] Such a man will "typically be a weaker person" who, on account of his incessantly warring drives, will crave a cessation of hostilities. He will also harbor a notion of happiness that encompasses rest, stasis, inner harmony, and "the 'Sabbath of Sabbaths,' to speak with the holy rhetorician Augustine, who was himself such a person." Do the above references to mixed races and "multiple lineages" suggest something other than a spiritual inheritance—a Zola-esque form of naturalism, perhaps?[16]

---

[15] White (1994, 67) contends that in passages such as these Nietzsche is "[c]learly ... using the language of race and heredity in order to describe something which transcends the narrowly biological. And indeed, I would suggest that the whole dialect of master and slave must also proceed along the same 'psychohistorical' or 'psychodramatic' register." *Pace* White, I find the meaning of these race/heredity passages to be far from clear. For example, if Nietzsche makes explicit reference to the 'body' and to 'drives' within the body, as he does in BGE 200, then he would appear to be describing something biological, which does not, of course, exclude the possibility that Nietzsche is also describing something which transcends the narrowly biological.

[16] See Zola's (1998, 1–6) 1873 preface to *Thérèse Raquin*.

In the second and third aphorisms, the lineage argument is impressed more forcibly upon the reader. The second aphorism is located in the book's final part, entitled 'What is Noble?':

> It is utterly impossible for a person *not* to have the qualities and propensities of his elders and ancestors in his body no matter how much appearances might speak against it. This is the problem of race. If you know anything about the ancestors, you can draw conclusions about the child. (BGE 264, KSA 5:219)

Whatever the vice or character flaw, continues BGE 264, it will just as surely be passed onto the child as "corrupted blood" [*verdebtes Blut*].[17] And no amount of education and culture, in what passes for education and culture in this "vulgar age" [*pöbelhaften Zeitalter*], can mask one's "lineage," one's "inherited vulgarity [*vererbten Pöbel*] in body and soul" (ibid.). Two things need to be noted here: the root word '*pöbel*' [rabble] in the adjective '*pöbelhaft*' [vulgar], and the homonymous adjectives '*verderbt*' [corrupted] and '*vererbt*' [inherited] which subtly link contaminated blood and rabble vulgarity, notwithstanding the analogical status of "corrupted blood."

The third aphorism, BGE 213 (KSA 5:147–149), is more ambiguous. It opens with the following statement, "In the last analysis, there is a rank order of psychic states which corresponds to the rank order of problems." These problems are of a philosophical nature, the solution to which, we are told, will never be found by plodding scholars and clumsy empiricists, but rather by those of spiritual height and heft—qualities which "predestine" [*vorherbestimmen*] them for finding such solutions. This predestination, continues Nietzsche, "has already been provided for in the primordial laws of things":

> You need to have been born for any higher world: to say it more clearly, you need to have been *bred* [*gezüchten*] for it: only your descent, your ancestry can give you a right to philosophy—taking that word in its highest sense. Even here, "bloodline" [*Geblüt*] is decisive. The preparatory labor of many generations is needed for a philosopher to come about; each of his virtues

---

[17] In order to make sense of Nietzsche's "overstress on 'breeding'—his notion of [human] drives as mainly inherited ('in the blood')," writes Richardson (1996, 48), "we must bear in mind his Lamarckism," i.e., the theory that an organism's physical changes could be inherited from its parents.

needs to have been individually acquired, nurtured, inherited, and incorporated [*einverleibt*]…

Note that the philosopher's "inherited" and "incorporated" virtues are the fruits of prior generations' acquisition and nurture—an incorporated inheritance which, in conjunction with the words 'born,' 'bred,' 'descent,' and 'ancestry,' seems to call into question the scare quotes around "bloodline."[18]

In the fourth aphorism, BGE 284 (KSA 5:231–232), Nietzsche presents his reader with a brief inventory of the types of virtue possessed by people like himself:

> To live with immense and proud composure; always beyond … to keep control of your four virtues: courage, insight, sympathy, solitude. Because solitude is a virtue for us, since it is a sublime inclination and impulse to cleanliness [*Reinlichkeit*], which shows that contact between people ("society") inevitably makes things unclean [*unvermeidlich-unreinlich zugehn muss*]. Somewhere, sometime, every community [*Gemeinheit*] makes people—"base" [*gemein*].

In this aphorism, the scare quoted adjective '*gemein*' is intended to flag the pun in '*Gemeinheit*.' The pun refers back to the homonymous wordplay '*reinlich*,' '*unvermeidlich*,' and '*unreinlich*' in the previous sentence, which in turn chimes with the subsequent '*gemein*,' thereby underscoring the uncleanliness of community.[19] What is lexically ambiguous here is whether the predicates 'clean' and 'unclean' are to be taken literally or figuratively.

---

[18] A crucial theme in Nietzsche's philosophical project, asserts Feldblyum (2021, 27–28), is the breeding of higher types—a theme that is all but anathema today and thus either downplayed or sanitized to make it more palatable to "our moral prejudices." "Throughout his corpus, Nietzsche displays significant interest in the history, design, and implementation of breeding programs for human beings manifesting specific physiological and psychological traits." A key component in any breeding program, notes Feldblyum (34), is selective marriage, enabling over the course of generations the promotion of desired traits and the reduction or elimination of undesired traits. Indeed, as attested to by numerous passages in the Nietzsche corpus, "the breeding and enhancement of aristocratic bloodlines through selective marriage" was one in which Nietzsche took a general interest.

[19] The uncleanliness of the community is not an idea that originated with Nietzsche. The pejorative English epithet 'the great unwashed' dates back to an 1829 article in *The Dublin Evening Mail*. https://wordhistories.net/2019/03/18/great-unwashed/.

Nietzsche uses the same semantic ploy in the fifth aphorism, BGE 20 (KSA 5:34–35). Here, he uses the homonymous syllables '*mein*' and '*meid*' to advance a similar argument for the inevitability of cross-contamination, or cross-insemination, within a community. And although the community referred to in BGE 20 is linguistic rather than social, Nietzsche again adverts to physiology and race, asserting that the family resemblance between Indian, Greek, and German philosophical systems ineluctably [*"ist es gar nicht zu vermeiden"*] arises from a "common [*gemeinsam*] philosophy of grammar." This grammar, he continues, is an expression of "*physiological* value judgments and racial conditioning," which, he claims, gives the lie to Locke's "superficial" account of the origin of ideas. Accordingly, "[p]hilosophers of the Ural-Altaic language group (where the concept of the subject is the most poorly developed) are more likely to 'see the world' differently, and to be found on paths different from those taken by the Indo-German or Muslims."

ESSENTIALIZING THE NOBLE AND THE COMMON

On the one hand, Nietzsche's antithetical epithets 'noble' and 'common,' 'master' and 'slave,' 'higher' and 'herd' can be viewed as nothing more than expressions of personal taste or prejudice. This line of reasoning is supported by Nietzsche's relentless epithets 'common,' 'herd,' 'slave,' and 'rabble,' and his citing of "disgust" [*Ekel*] as one of the defining traits of the higher types with regard to the lower types. On the other hand, the argument for taste and perspectivism is harder to sustain in light of Nietzsche's declaration that the traits of these two diametrically opposed ranks are instinctive.

Throughout BGE, one encounters the collocations 'rabble instinct' (BGE 204, KSA 5:129), 'herd instinct' (BGE 199, KSA 5:119, BGE 201, KSA 5:122 & BGE 202, KSA 5:124), 'democratic instinct' (BGE 22, KSA 5:37), 'religious instinct' (BGE 53, KSA 5:73 & BGE 58, KSA 5:76), and the "*English* instinct to spend Sundays in tedium with a *te deum* so that the English people would unconsciously lust for their week- and workdays" (BGE 189, KSA 5:189). All of these are used by Nietzsche to denote the timidity and industriousness of the ignoble type. In contradistinction to these instincts, Nietzsche sets "*an instinct for rank*" (BGE 263, KSA 5:217) and the kindred instincts of retribution (BGE 265, KSA 5:220), manliness, conquest, and domination (BGE 62, KSA 5:82). Accompanying these purportedly noble and common traits is a mutual hostility between the two ranks. The "plebeian" stratum, with its "instincts of mediocrity" (BGE 206, KSA 5:134), is hostile towards "all privilege and autocracy" (BGE 22, KSA 5:37). By contrast, "the noble soul," holding the unshakable belief that "other beings will, by nature [*von Natur*], have to be sacrificed [*opfern*] to them" (BGE 265, KSA 5:219), "instinctively" seeks its own secret, solitary sanctuary as far away as possible from "the animal, the commonplace, the 'norm'" (BGE 26, KSA 5:44).

The adjectives 'instinctive' [*instinktiv*] and 'fundamental/basic' [*Grund*] are used synonymously in BGE. What is particularly noteworthy in this regard is the neologistic compound nouns that Nietzsche builds onto the root word '*Grund*' and which appear to be synonymous with the noun '*Grundtriebe*' [basic drives] (BGE 6, KSA 5:20). Three of these compound nouns, namely, "*Grundgeschmack*" [fundamental taste] (BGE 239, KSA 5:175), "*Grundhang*" [basic tendency] (BGE 44, KSA 5:61), and "*Grundfeindschaft*" [fundamental hostility] (BGE 260, KSA 5:210), are linked to a "*demokratischen Hang*" [democratic tendency] in general (BGE 239, KSA 5:175) and a "*plebejischen Grundgeschmack*" [plebeian taste] in particular (BGE 14, KSA 5:28). The latter "instinctively" follows an "eternally popular sensualism" (ibid.), while the former is driven by the "herd-desirability" [*Heerde-Wünschbarkeit*] of green-pasture happiness evoked by the popular slogans "'equal rights' and 'sympathy for all that suffers'" (BGE 44, KSA 5:61–62). In contradistinction to these democratic proclivities is the noble soul's "*Grundgewissheit*" [fundamental certainty] about itself (BGE 287, KSA 5:233) and its "*Grundglaube*" [fundamental belief] that the "*gemeine Volk*" [common people] are liars (BGE 260, KSA 5:209). In a similar vein, "the essential feature of a good, healthy aristocracy" is said to be its *Grundglaube* that countless people have to be sacrificed and "shrunk into incomplete human beings" in order to serve as the "substructure and framework for raising an exceptional type of being up to its higher duty and to a higher state of *being*" (BGE 258, KSA 206–207). More astonishing, even, than the latter assertion is the analogy Nietzsche alights upon of the Javanese climbing plant, which wraps its tendrils around the trunk of an oak tree and in the fullness of time "unfold[s] its highest crown of foliage" into the open light (ibid.). The analogy suggests a natural order in which the coarse, earthy, solid mass of people (the tree) is merely the means by which the refined aristocrats (the delicate tendrils) fulfill their highest duty, namely, to realize "a higher state of *being*."

Nietzsche uses a similar plant analogy in BGE 259 (KSA 5:207–208). In this aphorism, he argues that exploitation is at bottom an organic function and thus in the natural order of things—hence his contemptuous scare quotes around the word 'exploitation,' a word historically freighted with opprobrious moral and political connotations, and his dual emphasis on the non-scare quoted words 'essence' and 'primal fact':

> "Exploitation" does not belong to a corrupted or imperfect primitive society: it belongs to the *essence* [*Wesen*] of being alive as a fundamental organic function; it is a result of the actual [*eigentlich*] will to power, which is just the will of life.—Although this is an innovation at the level of theory,—at the level of reality, it is the *primal fact* of all history. Let us be honest with ourselves to this extent at least!

In other words, if will to power is a metaphysical principle, which the stressed words *essence* and *primal* arguably suggest, then it is axiomatically the fundamental driving force of *all* history. The inherent aggression of this will to power is clearly set out in the passage immediately prior to the one cited above and is adduced by Nietzsche as the ontological principal underpinning class oppression and exploitation:

> life itself is *essentially* [*wesentlich*] a process of appropriating, injuring, overpowering the alien and the weaker, oppressing, being harsh, imposing your own form, incorporating, and at least, the very least, exploiting,—but what is the point of always using words that have been stamped with slanderous intentions from time immemorial? Even a body [*Körper*] within which ... particular individuals treat each other as equal (which happens in every healthy aristocracy): if this body is living and not dying, it must itself [*muss selber*] treat all other bodies in just those ways that the individuals it contains *refrain* from treating each other. It will have to be [*sein müssen*] the embodied [*leibhaftig*] will to power, it will want to grow, spread, grab, win dominance,—not out of any morality or immorality, but because it is *alive*, and because life *is* precisely will to power.

What is most striking here is the ambiguous signification of *Körper*, which, in common with its English equivalent, can refer to both the corporeal body and the body politic. In light of the passage's organic framing, the word appears to be functioning as a pun: Given its will to power essence, the healthy aristocracy qua highest stratum of the body politic *naturally/ organically* exploits and dominates the "other bodies" comprising the lower or slave strata (see BGE 225, cited in the 'Slave' subsection above) of the body politic.

Another reference to will to power can be found in BGE 22 (KSA 5:37). In this aphorism, Nietzsche ridicules the physicists' dictum that nature conforms to natural laws. Rehearsing the Kantian epistemological stance in Nietzsche's 1873 essay 'On Truth and Lies in a Nonmoral Sense,' namely that "the eternal consistency, omnipresence, and fallibility of the laws of nature" is a human invention, or in Nietzsche's heightened rhetoric an "arrogant" anthropomorphic lie (see Chap. 2), BGE 22 dismisses this posited conformity to natural laws as a "naïve humanitarian distortion of meaning." This distortion, contends Nietzsche, serves the dual purpose of accommodating "the democratic instincts of the modern soul!" and disguising the democratic instinct's natural hostility towards the autocratic instinct. Note the shift in emphasis here, from Nietzsche's 1873 'truth and lie' moralizing of erroneous epistemological assumptions to a grounding of these assumptions in a 'democratic instinct.' Against these erroneous interpretations, Nietzsche posits as the ground of nature "a tyrannically ruthless and pitiless execution of power claims." Even the use of the word 'tyranny,' adds Nietzsche, is a woefully inadequate metaphor for "the unequivocal and unconditional nature of all 'will to power.'" Of particular note here is the scare quoted phrase 'will to power'—a reminder to the reader that it, too, is a woefully inadequate metaphor for what Nietzsche alleges to be the unequivocal and unconditional ground of being, and what I would argue is a Nietzschean version of the Kantian *Ding an sich*.[20]

I shall end this chapter with aphorism 257 (KSA 5:205–206), which opens the BGE chapter 'What is Noble?' The aphorism begins with the confident assertion that "Every enhancement so far in the type 'man' has been the work of an aristocratic society—and that is how it will be, again and again, since this sort of society believes in a long ladder of rank order and value distinctions between men, and in some sense needs slavery." Nietzsche goes on to affirm that this sort of society, constituted by the "noble caste," originated in "the barbarian caste."

> Men whose nature was still natural, barbarians in every terrible sense of the word, predatory people who still possessed an unbroken strength of will and

---

[20] My Kantian interpretation of Nietzsche's 'will to power' is similar to the way in which Hinman (1982, 196) interprets Nietzsche's *Birth of Tragedy* claim that Dionysian art has a greater claim to truth than Apollonian art because the former brings the spectator closer to the primal nature of existence. "Insofar as he identifies this Dionysian domain as possessing some type of ontological priority," writes Hinman, "Nietzsche seems to be continuing—albeit in a somewhat unusual manner—the Kantian tradition of the *Ding an sich* with all of its attendant problems."

lust for power, threw themselves on weaker, more civilized, more peaceful races of tradesmen perhaps, or cattle breeders ...

Embedded in this passage is the same delineation of will to power as the "tyrannical" one in BGE 259 (mentioned above). But whereas the barbarians' lust for power over the weaker races expressed itself in physical strength, the same lust for power has evolved within the noble caste into a psychic "supremacy." This supremacy is consonant with the noble soul's "*pathos of distance*" which, according to Nietzsche, grows out of [*erwachsen*] "the ingrained [*eingefleischt*] differences between stations" (BGE 257). Note here the adjective '*eingefleischt*,' from the Middle High German *ingevleischet*, meaning to make flesh or to make incarnate. And in conjunction with Nietzsche's multiple references to 'instinctive,' 'fundamental,' and 'will to power,' the adjective 'ingrained' suggests that the "long ladder of rank order and value distinctions between men" (ibid.) is something innate.

What this chapter has sought to demonstrate is the danger of being swept along by the sheer force of Nietzsche's rhetoric. The cumulative effect of his mind-numbing mantra of adjectival epithets, compound nouns, an inborn order of rank, and essentializing adjectives such as 'ingrained,' 'inborn,' 'instinctive,' and 'inherited,' is to lull the reader into a stupor of uncritical acquiescence in notions that we would otherwise find highly distasteful.

References

Ackerman, Robert John. 1990. *Nietzsche: A Frenzied Look*. Amherst: The University of Massachusetts Press.

Cauchi, Francesca. 2022. *Zarathustra's Moral Tyranny: Spectres of Kant, Hegel and Feuerbach*. Edinburgh: Edinburgh University Press.

Constâncio, João. 2011. Instinct and language in Nietzsche's *Beyond Good and Evil*. In *Nietzsche on Instinct and Language*, ed. João Constâncio and Maria João Mayer Branco, 80–116. Berlin/Boston: de Gruyter.

Conway, Daniel. 1994. Parastrategesis, or: Rhetoric for decadents. *Philosophy & Rhetoric* 27 (3): 179–201.

Derrida, Jacques. 1984. *The Ear of the Other: Otobiography, Transference, Translation*. Trans. Peggy Kamuf. New York: Schocken Books.

Drapela, Nathan. 2020. A matter of taste: Nietzsche and the structure of affective response. *Inquiry* 63 (1): 85–103.

Feldblyum, Leonard. 2021. The responsibility to be hard: Comments on Ken Gemes's 'The Biology of Evil.' *The Journal of Nietzsche Studies* 52 (1): 26–39.

Gemes, Ken. 1992. Nietzsche's critique of truth. *Philosophy and Phenomenological Research* 52 (1): 47–65.

Hargis, Jill. 2010. (Dis)embracing the herd: A look at Nietzsche's shifting views of the people and the individual. *History of Political Thought* 31.3: 475–507.

Hinman, Lawrence M. 1982. Nietzsche, metaphor, and truth. *Philosophy and Phenomenological Research* 43 (2): 179–199.

Hume, David. 1960. *A Treatise of Human Nature*. Oxford: Clarendon Press.

Leiter, Brian. 2014. *Nietzsche on Morality*. 2nd ed. London: Routledge.

Lupo, Luca. 2006. *Le Colombe Dello Scettico, Riflessioni Di Nietzsche Sulla Coscienza Negli Anni 1880-1888*. Pisa: Edizioni ETZ.

May, Simon. 1999. *Nietzsche's Ethics and his War on 'Morality.'* New York: Oxford University Press.

Migotti, Mark. 2006. Slave morality, Socrates, and the bushmen: A critical introduction to *On the Genealogy of Morality, Essay I*. In *Nietzsche's On the Genealogy of Morals: Critical Essays*, ed. Christa Davis Acampora, 109–129. Lanham: Rowman & Littlefield.

Mitchell, Jonathan. 2017. Nietzsche on taste: Epistemic privilege and anti-realism. *Inquiry* 60: 31–65.

Nehamas, Alexander. 1985. *Nietzsche: Life as Literature*. Cambridge: Harvard University Press.

Nietzsche, Friedrich. 1992. *Philosophy and Truth: Selections from Nietzsche's Notebooks of the Early 1870's*. Trans. Daniel Breazeale. Atlantic Highlands: Humanities Press.

———. 2001a. *The Gay Science*. Trans. Josefine Nauckhoff. New York: Cambridge University Press.

———. 2001b. *Thus Spoke Zarathustra: A Book for All and None*. Trans. Adrian Del Caro. New York: Cambridge University Press.

———. 2002. *Beyond Good and Evil: Prelude to a Philosophy of the Future*. Trans. Judith Norman. New York: Cambridge University Press.

———. 2006. *Daybreak: Thoughts on the Prejudices of Morality*. Trans. R. J. Hollingdale. Cambridge: Cambridge University Press.

———. 2007a. *Human, All Too Human: A Book for Free Spirits*. Trans. R. J. Hollingdale. Cambridge: Cambridge University Press.

———. 2007b. *On the Genealogy of Morality*. Trans. Carol Diethe. New York: Cambridge University Press.

Poellner, Peter. 2000. *Nietzsche and Metaphysics*. New York: Oxford University Press.

Richardson, John. 1996. *Nietzsche's System*. New York: Oxford University Press.

Solomon, Robert C. 1994. One hundred years of *ressentiment*: Nietzsche's *Genealogy of Morals*. In *Nietzsche, Genealogy, Morality*, ed. Richard Schacht, 95–126. Berkeley: University of California Press.

———. 1996. Nietzsche *ad hominem*: Perspectivism, personality and *ressentiment*. In *The Cambridge Companion to Nietzsche*, ed. Bernd Magnus and Kathleen M. Higgins, 180–222. Cambridge: Cambridge University Press.

White, Richard. 1994. The return of the master: An interpretation of Nietzsche's *Genealogy of Morals*. In *Nietzsche, Genealogy, Morality*, ed. Richard Schacht, 63–75. Berkeley: University of California Press. https://wordhistories. net/2019/03/18/great-unwashed/.

Zola, Émile. 1998. *Thérèse Raquin*. Trans. Andrew Rothwell. Oxford: Oxford University Press.

CHAPTER 5

From Malice to Magnanimity

Twilight of the Idols or How to Philosophize with a Hammer (1888)

Abstract This chapter reads *Twilight of the Idols* against *Beyond Good and Evil* to reveal a shift in tone from the vitriol of the earlier text to the good-natured, light-hearted chaffing of the later work, despite *Twilight*'s subtitle 'How to Philosophize with a Hammer' and despite the text's closing injunction—borrowed from the pity-hobbled Zarathustra—to "*become hard!*" (Z3 'On Old and New Law Tables' 29, KSA 4:268). Thus, while Nietzsche's rhetorical arsenal is still in combat mode, his objective is no longer to slash and burn but to jape and jibe. A glaring exception to this tonal shift is 'The Problem of Socrates,' an early *Twilight* chapter in which Socrates' reputed ugliness precipitates a return to the arguably ugly animus of *Beyond Good and Evil*. The following chapter is divided into two halves: The first maps out Nietzsche's path from the malice of *Beyond Good and Evil* to the magnanimity of *Twilight*, while the second examines the philological bad faith in Nietzsche's elaborate rhetorical ruses aimed at proving to the reader that Socrates was a decadent.

Keywords Nietzsche • *Twilight of the Idols* • Decadence • Socrates • Lombroso • Criminal anthropology • *Ad hominem*

INTRODUCTION

Twilight of the Idols can be read as an embellishment—a parergon, if you will—of *Beyond Good and Evil.* Both texts exhibit similar structural and thematic traits and share the same basic premise. Structurally, BGE and *Twilight* respectively comprise nine and ten titled parts [*Hauptstück*] (for the sake of clarity, I shall use 'chapter' for part, and 'segment' for the numbered subsections within each part); both texts contain one chapter consisting solely of epigrams; and both end with a short piece of verse or quasi-verse (BGE ends with one of Nietzsche's blushingly poor poems, while *Twilight* ends with an excerpt from *Zarathustra*). Common themes include morality and religion, German thought and culture, and what Nietzsche judges to be the prejudices, errors, or—more magnanimously—idiosyncrasies of philosophers. Philosophical errors include causality, binary oppositions (e.g., good and evil, altruism and self-interest), *causa sui*, absolute knowledge, the Kantian *Ding an sich*, and the will as a rationally determined cause of action rather than the end product of a complex multiplicity of feelings and drives. The core premise of both works is the anti-realist claim that all value judgments are rooted in and hence expressions of the affects (see the section entitled 'Taste, Affects, and Epistemic Privilege' in Chap. 4).

Notwithstanding the above commonalities, my focus in the first section of this chapter is on what sets *Twilight* and BGE apart. This, I shall argue, is *Twilight*'s overall magnanimity and an appreciable softening of tone—notwithstanding the work's subtitle, 'How to Philosophize with a Hammer.' In the second section of the chapter, I will showcase Nietzsche's art of reading badly, which is particularly egregious in the *Twilight* chapter entitled 'The Problem of Socrates.' It is a reading, moreover, that in its rhetorical sophistry is as impudent and arbitrary as that which Nietzsche excoriates in Christian hermeneutics (discussed at the start of the second section of this chapter).

LEARNING TO SEE AND TO WITHHOLD JUDGMENT

Twilight's lightness of touch[1] recalls the sun-lit warmth of a Genoan spring that in Nietzsche's retrospective appraisal radiates from the pages of *Daybreak*: "This *affirmative* book saves its light, its love, its tenderness for

[1] Dannhauser (1974, 203) draws our attention to the "antidogmatic" tone of the first chapter of *Twilight*, 'Maxims and Arrows,' evidenced by the latter's punctuation: "More than one-third of the aphorisms in this section end in dots or dashes or question marks; more than two-thirds contain such punctuation. The aphorisms, which are generalizations, are to be taken as stimulating insights rather than as final truths."

bad things alone, it gives them back their 'soul,' a good conscience, the high right and *privilege* to exist" (EH 'Daybreak' 1, KSA 6:330). The same affirmative stance is implicit in the following *Twilight* delineation of a less reactive, less judgmental, less rebarbative, hammer-hard critical method:

> Learning to *see*—getting your eyes used to calm, to patience, to letting things come to it; postponing judgment, learning to encompass and take stock of an individual case from all sides. This is the *first* preliminary schooling for spirituality: *not* to react immediately to a stimulus, but instead to take control of the inhibiting, excluding instincts. (TI 'Germans' 6, KSA 6:108)

To borrow Nietzsche's military metaphors, the "gunpowder" (EH 'Daybreak' 1, KSA 6:329) of BGE has been decommissioned and replaced with an alternative strategy of "cheerful" (see TI Preface, KSA 6:57–58; TI 'Germans' 3, KSA 6:105–106; and EH 'Twilight' 1, KSA 6:354), light-hearted "skirmishes," the highest incidence of which occurs in the late *Twilight* chapter 'Skirmishes of an Untimely Man.'

Comprising fifty-one aphorisms and by far the longest chapter in the text, 'Skirmishes' takes playful pot-shots at illustrious men. The chapter opens with the following rogues' gallery of caricatured philosophers and writers:

> *My impossible ones.*—*Seneca*: or the toreador of virtue. —*Rousseau*: or the return to nature *in impuris naturalibus. Schiller*: or the moral trumpeter of Säckingen. —*Dante*: or the hyena who *writes poetry* in tombs.—*Kant*: or cant as intelligible character.—*Victor Hugo*: or the lighthouse on the sea of nonsense ... *Carlyle*: or pessimism as coughed-up lunch. —*John Stuart Mill*: or insulting clarity. —*Les frères de Goncourt*: or the two Ajaxes fighting with Homer. Music by Offenbach. —*Zola*: or "the joy of stinking". (TI 'Skirmishes' 1, KSA 6:112)

The aphorism's title immediately sets the tone for the chapter as a whole. Cheerful, mischievous, and humorously irreverent, its tone could not be further removed from the splenetic insults and rogues' gallery of 'slave,' 'herd,' and 'rabble' types in BGE—a comparison which calls to mind Nietzsche's BGE quip regarding the "subtler poison" of Christianity with which the English treat the "cruder poison" of their spleen and "alcoholic dissipation" (BGE 252, KSA 5:195–196). Compare, too, Nietzsche's *Twilight* reference to Thomas à Kempis' book *Imitatio Christi*, which "exudes a scent of the eternal feminine, which is fine if you happen to be

French—or a Wagnerian" (TI 'Skirmishes' 4, KSA 6:113), with his vicious, venomous cluster of references in BGE 30 (KSA 5:48–49) to the foul-smelling books, the small-people-stench, and the stink of places where the common people [*"das Volk"*] eat, drink, and worship. Or, to give another example, compare *Twilight*'s ironic depiction of the English propensity to cling ever more tightly to Christian morality in the absence of a Christian God as typical *"English* consistency" (TI 'Skirmishes' 5, KSA 6:113), with BGE's reference to the English Utilitarians' "vomit-inducing" [*Brechmittel*] creed of "'general welfare'" (BGE 228, KSA 6:165).

The only way to cut through the "cant" and bland vapidity of the English Utilitarians, writes Nietzsche in BGE, is "to sour it with malice" (BGE 228, KSA 5:164). But as we saw in the preceding chapter, his malice sours considerably more than Utilitarian morality. And despite avowals to the contrary, his malice in BGE does not always proceed from the "[g]enuine honesty" of free spirits (BGE 227, KSA 5:162–163). For if free spirits are those whose "self-overcoming of morality" has given them the right to be "the most malicious consciences of the day" (BGE 32, KSA 5:51), and whose *"duty*" it is "to squint as maliciously as possible out of every abyss of mistrust" so that the errors, prejudices, and assumptions of past thinkers can be brought to light (BGE 34, KSA 5:52–53), then such free spirits ought to be free of the kind of prejudices and assumptions on display in BGE (see Chap. 4).

One of the greatest errors of past thinkers, avers Nietzsche, was the attempt to ground moral sentiment in a "'science of morals'" based exclusively on (culturally freighted) moral acts culled from "their surroundings, their class, their church, their *Zeitgeist*" (BGE 186, KSA 5:105–107). Citing Schopenhauer as a case in point and wryly noting the latter's "almost admirable innocence," Nietzsche describes as "fatuously false and sentimental" Schopenhauer's attempt to ground all morality in philanthropic compassion (ibid.). Similarly, in *Twilight*, Schopenhauer's attempt to press "the great self-affirmation of the 'will to live'" into the service of a nihilistic devaluation of life is reviled as "maliciously ingenious"—a different kind of malice, presumably, from the one reserved for those who have overcome morality. Nietzsche, however, instantly retracts the charge of malice and, heeding his own counsel, withholds judgment until he has viewed Schopenhauer's case "from all sides" (see TI 'Germans' 6 citation at the start of this section). "[O]n closer inspection," he continues, Schopenhauer's nihilistic life-denial was merely symptomatic of the Christian worldview to which he was heir and in spite of which

Schopenhauer "knew how to *approve* of what Christianity had rejected," namely, the great cultural facts of humanity such as art, heroism, genius, beauty, tragedy, and knowledge (TI 'Skirmishes' 21, KSA 6:125).

Indeed, what Nietzsche specifically objects to in the case of Schopenhauer is the way in which he co-opted the aforesaid cultural facts to further a nihilistic goal—i.e., the denial of the will—and to provide a path to "'redemption'" (TI 'Skirmishes' 21, KSA 6:125). One such redemption was Schopenhauer's view of beauty as a "momentary redemption" from the will as manifested in man's primordial sex drive. "Bizarre saint!" indulgently exclaims the philosopher of will to power; "all beauty is a temptation to procreate … this is precisely the *proprium* of its effect, from the lowest sensuality to the highest spirituality" ('Skirmishes' 22, KSA 6:125–126). "Another bizarre saint!" for Nietzsche, especially in matters of beauty and sexual desire, is Plato, whom Nietzsche facetiously quotes as saying, "there could never have been a Platonic philosophy without such beautiful young men in Athens" ('Skirmishes' 23, KSA 6:126). (Nietzsche's predilection for the rhetorical figure of dialogue will be discussed in the second section of this chapter.)

Other historical figures mentioned in *Twilight* are treated with similar affability, their tics and foibles the occasion for an ironic or jesting parenthetic quip rather than a malicious thrust. Take, for example, Thomas Carlyle's inner conflict between "yearning for a strong faith *and* the feeling that he is not up to the task (—which makes him a typical romantic!)" ('Skirmishes' 12, KSA 6:119), or Darwin's account of the species evolving towards ever more perfect forms—a view deemed by Nietzsche to be conclusively refuted by the fact that the weak, with their greater cunning and numbers, have become the masters of the strong. "Darwin forgot about intelligence (—typically English!)" ('Skirmishes' 14, KSA 6:120–121). Nietzsche is also appreciably less malicious towards Wagner in *Twilight* than he is in BGE. What in the latter text is the "murky howling," "self-disemboweling," and "nun-eyed Ave-chiming" of Wagner's *Parsifal* (BGE 256, KSA 5:204), is quietly dismissed in *Twilight* as "*pure foolishness*" [*reine Thorheit*] ('Skirmishes' 30, KSA 6:130). Note here Nietzsche's wordplay on Wagner's Schopenhauer-imbued depiction of Parsifal as the "pure fool" who understands through pity (see Act 1 chorus: "*Durch Mitleid wissend, der reine Tor*"). Another type of foolishness is what Nietzsche refers to as the "*niaiserie allemande*" [German silliness] of sensing "beautiful souls" in the Greeks while completely overlooking the Dionysian "will to power," which for Nietzsche constitutes the "overflowing Hellenic instinct" (TI 'What I Owe the Ancients' 3–4, KSA 6:157–158).

An overflowing instinct is not an attribute Nietzsche ever associated with his compatriots. On the contrary, he devotes a late chapter in both BGE and *Twilight* to the diagnosis of this German deficiency. But whereas the BGE chapter, 'Peoples and Fatherlands,' bristles with missiles directed at the collective German head,[2] the *Twilight* chapter, 'What the Germans Lack,' is marked by restraint and fairness. The latter begins with a generous appraisal ("I want to be fair to the Germans") of German qualities, namely, their fortitude and self-respect, their sense of reciprocal duty, their "hereditary sense of moderation that needs to be spurred rather than curbed," and their lack of contempt for opponents. It then moves on to the Germans' purported lack of instinctual superfluity and the manifestations of this lack, both of which are adduced in a calm and measured tone. The first cited manifestation is political, "'*Deutschland, Deutschland über Alles*'; this, I'm afraid, was the end of German philosophy"—that and the "[d]amned instinct of mediocrity!" (TI 'Germans' 1, KSA 6:103–104). Note how the sudden flare of impatience is swiftly doused by the exclamation mark. The second manifestation is cultural, namely, "our constipated, constipating" German music, the heavy, yeasty, stupefying effect of which is wittily attributed to the beer-addled German intellect ('Germans' 2, KSA 6:104). And the third manifestation is educational: On the one hand, the "severe helotism" of German scholarship ('Germans' 3, KSA 6:105), and on the other, the "indecent" haste with which Germany's "democratized" system of higher education seeks to turn hordes of young men into serviceable material for the civil service ('Germans' 5, KSA 6:107–108).

The measure and moderation evinced in the first five segments of 'What the Germans Lack' is tacitly acknowledged in the sixth, in Nietzsche's self-characterization as a type "which is *affirmative* and only reluctantly and parenthetically has anything to do with dispute or criticism" (TI 'Germans' 6, KSA 6:108). He makes a similar remark earlier in the text, "We [immoralists] do not negate easily, we stake our honor on being *affirmative*" (TI 'Morality' 6, KSA 6:87). What are we to make of these two assertions? Are they frank or disingenuous? I would argue that these two "*affirmative*"

---

[2] A representative sample of the German targets in 'Peoples and Fatherlands' is their "boorish indifference to 'taste'" (BGE 244, KSA 5:186); their high fever nationalism, manifest in "anti-French stupidity one moment and the anti-Jewish stupidity the next, now the anti-Polish stupidity, now the Christian Romantic, the Wagnerian, the Teutonic, the Prussian" (BGE 251, KSA 5:192); and the "Germanization or vulgarization" of taste in French music, as a result of Wagner's aforesaid "Christian Romantic" excesses (BGE 254, KSA 5:198–199).

self-evaluations are given in earnest. Not only is the work's overall tone magnanimous; its stated goal in the preface is to *"sound out idols"* with a tuning fork—despite the text's subtitle, 'How to philosophize with a hammer' (the titular-textual misalignment flagged in Chap. 2), and despite the preface's *"great declaration of war"* against current and *"eternal* idols" (TI Pref., KSA 6:58).

Sounding out idols with a tuning fork is evident in the opening segment of 'Morality as Anti-Nature'—a subject upon which Nietzsche is generally the least restrained. Opting for irreverent humor (the tuning fork) over naked aggression (the hammer), he begins by referring to the Christian practice of "castrating" the passions rather than "spiritualizing" [*vergeistigen*] them. The verb 'castrating' is made to do double service here as a rhetorical goad and an implicit reference to Christianity's demonization of sexuality. Hence Nietzsche's quip on the Sermon on the Mount, "where, incidentally, things are certainly not viewed *from a higher perspective.* When it comes to sexuality, for instance, it says: 'if your eye offends you, pluck it out' [Matt. 5:29]: fortunately, Christians do not follow this rule." Nietzsche then segues into facetious wordplay, declaring that the reason why the church never asks itself how a desire might be "spiritualized, beautified, deified" is because "the first church even fought *against* the 'intelligent' [*die 'Intelligenten'*] for the sake of the 'poor in spirit [*Geist*]': How could we expect it to have waged an intelligent [*einen intelligenten*] war on the passions?" ('Morality' 1, KSA 6:82–83).

Nietzsche's avowed reluctance to mire himself in "dispute and criticism" is also very much to the fore in the fifth segment of 'Morality as Anti-Nature.' The latter's critical focus is the root cause of Christianity's "sacrilegious" revolt against life, the kind of revolt, adds Nietzsche, that is "practically sacrosanct for Christian morality." Note here the deployment of Christian terms to critique Christianity—a distinctive feature of Nietzsche's rhetorical style, albeit one which I have not had occasion to flag before now. However, notwithstanding the "absurdity" and "deceitfulness" of the Christian revolt, Nietzsche recognizes that any condemnation of life by the living is ultimately "only the symptom of a certain type of life." He also recognizes that the question of whether a condemnation of life is justified is not one we can ever answer, for in order to do so "you would need to be both *outside* life and as familiar with life as someone, anyone, everyone who has ever lived." In short, "the problem of the *value* of life ... is inaccessible to us" ('Morality' 5, KSA 6:86). The same applies to any fixed concept of "*ecce homo,*" which in the final segment of 'Morality' is contrasted with life's "enchanting abundance of types, a lavish profusion of forms in change and at play." Note how far removed this celebration of diversity is from BGE's rank order of types, just as Nietzsche's gentle chiding of the moralist who demands that "people should be *different from the way they are*" ('Morality' 6, KSA 6:86–87) is a far cry from his pejorative epithets in BGE.

It is worth pausing here to note that the BGE epithets 'common,' 'slave,' and 'herd' rarely appear in *Twilight* and, when they do appear, it is invariably without malice. In *Twilight*, the adjective 'common' is used to denote the abovementioned democratization of higher education in Germany, which in Nietzsche's view has reduced to a "commonplace" what was once "higher" and a "privilege" (TI 'Germans' 5, KSA 6:107–108). The only slaves to be met with in the text are the workers. Newly liberated from their former slavery and emboldened by their new-found right to unionize and to vote, they now find their existence to be an injustice. Unsurprisingly so, remarks Nietzsche. After all, he retorts, it is simply a question of forward planning: "If you will an end, you have to will the means too: if you want slaves, then it is stupid to train them to be masters" ('Skirmishes' 40, KSA 6:142–143). Lastly, there are just two iterations of the word 'herd' in *Twilight*, both in the same segment. In this segment, the "*herd animalization*" of man, over which Nietzsche froths and fumes in BGE, is held to be a paradoxical effect of liberalism ('Skirmishes' 38, KSA 6:139–140). Here, instead of reviling liberalism's "brutalizing process of turning humanity into stunted little animals with equal rights and equal claims" (BGE 203, KSA 5:127–128), Nietzsche dispassionately interprets the demand for equal rights as symptomatic of "a *declining* stratum of society" ('Skirmishes' 34, KSA 6:132). He attributes the same decline to the entire discipline of sociology in England and France, reasoning that if the latter has only ever experienced "the *decaying forms* of society," it will "innocently" use its "own instinct of decay as the *norm* for sociological value judgments." In the same way, our "weaker, more sensitive, and more vulnerable [constitution] … will necessarily give rise to a *considerate* morality" ('Skirmishes' 37, KSA 5:136–139).

The instinct of decay, however, is not confined to modernity. In the second chapter of *Twilight*, 'The Problem of Socrates,' Nietzsche discerns the same instinct in the ugliness of Socrates' face. But whereas in the 'Skirmishes' chapter (discussed above), the emphasis is on the innocence of this instinctual decay and of the resulting errors in reasoning and judgment (e.g., Schopenhauer's "admirable innocence" in attempting to ground all morality in compassion or in imagining that beauty is a redemption from the lusty will rather than the will's most potent stimulus), the emphasis in

'The Problem of Socrates' is on the 'ugly' side of decadence. Not only is the literal ugliness of Socrates' face cited as symptomatic of an underlying decay, but also as being symptomatic of "his emblematic *rachitic spite* [*Rachitiker-Bosheit*]" (TI 'Socrates' 4, KSA 6:69). Note here that the latter predicate is not only emphasized but made into a compound noun, which, like the profusion of compound nouns in BGE, seems to say more about Nietzsche's spite than it does about the objects of his spite. Instead of postponing judgment and suppressing instinctive reactions, instead of adopting a less jaundiced way of seeing—the type of seeing that distinguishes *Twilight* from BGE, Nietzsche judges "everything" about Socrates to be "exaggerated, *buffo*, a caricature—and at the same time, hidden, subterranean, and full of ulterior motives." But as I shall argue in the following section, everything about 'The Problem of Socrates' chapter is similarly "exaggerated, *buffo*, a caricature … full of ulterior motives."

THE ART OF READING BADLY

Nietzsche's attempt to establish Socrates' decadence on the basis of his ugliness is astonishing on a number of levels. First, it exhibits none of *Twilight*'s characteristic magnanimity. Second, it displays the very traits— "exaggerated, *buffo*, a caricature"—that Nietzsche despises in Socrates. And third, it bears the marks of the kind of philological dishonesty that Nietzsche detects and deplores in the medieval scholastics:

> How little Christianity educates the sense of honesty and justice can be gauged fairly well from the character of its scholars' writings: they present their conjectures as boldly as if they were dogmas and are rarely in any honest perplexity over the interpretation of a passage in the Bible. Again and again they say "I am right, for it is written" and then follows an interpretation of such impudent arbitrariness that a philologist who hears it is caught between rage and laughter and asks himself: Is it possible? Is this honorable? Is it even decent? How much dishonesty in this matter is still practiced in Protestant pulpits, how grossly the preacher exploits the advantage that no one is going to interrupt him here, how the Bible is pummeled and punched and the *art of reading badly* is in all due form imparted to the people. (D 84, KSA 3:79)

The remainder of the aphorism purports to give an example of Christian hermeneutics at its most dishonest. Instead, what is imparted to the reader is Nietzsche's own "art of reading badly"—a reading which counters the "philological farce" of interpreting the Old Testament as a fundamentally Christian text with the time-worn rhetorical farce of the straw man fallacy (see D 84, KSA 3:79–80[3]). And like the Protestant pulpiteer in D 84, Nietzsche's reading has the advantage of being secure against any kind of interruption mid-rhetorical flow. In the following critique, I aim to expose the bold conjectures, the "impudent" interpretations, and a general lack of justice and honesty in Nietzsche's straw man attempt to prove that Socrates was a decadent. Whether or not this dishonesty should be interpreted in *Twilight*'s spirit of magnanimity—e.g., as an 'innocent' symptom of Nietzsche's own instinct of decay—or as an innocuous example of *niaiserie allemande*, is a moot point.

The core premise of 'The Problem of Socrates,' and indeed of *Twilight* as a whole, is that all value judgments about life, be they positive or negative, are never true but merely symptomatic of an underlying physiology. Put simply, a robust physiology will generate positive judgments about life whereas a degenerating physiology will produce negative judgments about life. On the basis of this cause-effect argument, Nietzsche asserts that the negative judgment passed on life by all the great sages is a symptom of physiological decay or, to cite the exaggerated figure in 'The Problem of Socrates,' a symptom of "carrion" ('Socrates' 1, KSA 6:67). In other words, life-devaluation typifies *"declining types"* [*Niedergangs-Typen*] ('Socrates' 2, KSA 6:67). Accordingly, if Socrates' dying words, "I owe Asclepius a rooster,"[4] can be construed as a negative judgment on life, then Socrates is *ipso facto* a declining type. In order to justify such a construal, however, Nietzsche engages in a series of rhetorical ploys so heavy-handed that the chapter can be read as the direct inverse (ugly rather than beautiful) of what in a later chapter Nietzsche holds to be the *niaiserie allemande* of German scholars sensing "beautiful souls" in the Greeks (see TI 'Ancients' 3–4, KSA 6:157, quoted in the previous section of this chapter).

The first of these ploys is the rhetorical figure of dialogue. Nietzsche begins by converting Socrates' aforementioned Asclepius remark into two

---

[3] "[H]owever much the Jewish scholars protested, the Old Testament was supposed to speak of Christ and only of Christ, and especially of his Cross; wherever a piece of wood, a rod, a ladder, a twig, a tree, a willow, a staff is mentioned, it is supposed to be a prophetic allusion to the wood of the Cross; even the erection of the one-horned beast and the brazen serpent, even Moses spreading his arms in prayer, *even* the spits on which the Passover lamb was roasted—all allusions to the Cross and as it were preludes to it!" (D 84).

[4] "Crito, we owe a cock to Aesculapius. Pay it and do not neglect it," *Phaedo* (Plato 2005, 118).

consecutive, tendentious statements. The first, "living—that means being sick a long time," is a skewed interpretation of the original remark, while the second, "I owe Asclepius the Savior a rooster," is an edited version of the original: (TI 'Socrates' 1; KSA 6:67). Note the interpolated epithet 'the Savior'—a textbook example of question begging. Nietzsche follows this with more free-wheeling ventriloquy. In a confected internal monologue, Socrates is presented to us in (anomalous) confessional mode: "'Socrates is no doctor,' he said quietly to himself: 'death is the only doctor here ... Socrates was only sick for a long time ...'" ('Socrates' 12, KSA 6:73—ellipses in the original).[5]

The second rhetorical ploy that Nietzsche uses in prosecuting his claim that Socrates represents a declining type is the informal fallacy of *ad hominem*. "Socrates was descended from the lowest segment of society," declares Nietzsche; "Socrates was rabble [*Pöbel*]. We know, we can still see how ugly he was" ('Socrates' 3, KSA 6:68). The first thing to bear in mind here is that whereas in BGE the 'rabble' epithet is explicitly linked to the epithets 'common,' 'herd,' and 'slave,' in *Twilight* it is used solely in connection with Socrates and is directly linked to decay. That said, all five epithets share the same referent, namely, the lower classes and the instincts which drive them. As discussed in Chap. 4, these classes are typologically classified by Nietzsche on the basis of the "imaginary revenge" which the oppressed 'slave' type is said to direct towards the 'master' type. Whether Nietzsche sees this revenge in Socrates' *"absurdly rational"* over-reliance on reason—"a permanent state of *daylight* against all dark desires" ('Socrates' 10, KSA 6:72)—or in the *sans-culotte* garb of 'modern ideas' such as equality and fraternity, he regards it as the defining trait of the

---

[5] Ventriloquizing, i.e., the rhetorical figure of dialogue, is a favorite ruse of Nietzsche's. Here is a stellar example from *Daybreak*, "'Oh eternity! Oh that I had no soul! Oh that I had never been born! I am damned, damned, lost for ever. A week ago you could have helped me. But now it is all over. Now I belong to the Devil. I go with him to Hell. Break, break, poor hearts of stone! Will you not break? What more can be done for hearts of stone? I am damned that you may be saved! There he is! Yes, there he is! Come, kind Devil! Come!'" (D 77, KSA 3:76).

'rabble' or 'decadent' type.[6] However, when Socrates' ugliness is adduced as further proof of his rabble roots, Nietzsche's *ad hominem* attack mutates into an argument for predicating ugliness on interbreeding and, by implication, physiognomy on physiology.

Before proceeding to the alleged link between physiognomy and physiology, it is necessary to comment on the status of *ad hominem* in Nietzsche's work. In an outstanding article entitled 'Nietzsche *ad hominem*: Perspectivism, personality and *ressentiment*,' Solomon (1996, 188–217) convincingly demonstrates how Nietzsche's genealogical approach to philosophy—"that most difficult and embarrassing form of *backward inference* ... from every way of thinking and valuing to the commanding *need* behind it" (GS 370; KSA 33:621)—not only validates but necessitates the *ad hominem* form of argumentation. This so-called fallacy, argues Solomon (1996, 217), is not specious at all. On the contrary, the flawed reasoning denoted by the word 'fallacy' lies not in the *ad hominem* argument itself but in the supposition that "a philosophy or its arguments can be cut away from their moorings in the soul of the individual and his or her culture and treated, as they say, under the aspect of eternity." If, on the other hand, we endorse the veracity of Nietzsche's claim that all value judgments are rooted in the affects, then Nietzsche's genealogy is a sound interpretive method, "something of a protracted *ad hominem* argument writ large ... a kind of denuding, unmasking, stripping away pretensions of universality

---

[6] It could also be argued that Nietzsche's extraordinary rhetorical gambit in this chapter is itself a display of decadent *ressentiment*, given that Socrates was a philosopher whom Nietzsche admired and reviled in equal measure. Nehamas (1985, 24–38) provides an extended and illuminating account of the many ways in which Nietzsche's philosophical endeavors coincide with those of Socrates insofar as they are both "intensely personal thinkers, actively engaged in changing ... the moral quality of the life of the people around them." Nehamas goes so far as to claim that Nietzsche was "always in direct competition with Socrates" and cites in support of this claim the contrast between the former's "swaggering, polemical, self-conscious and self-aggrandizing" style and the latter's "ironic humility" and "arrogant self-effacement." Noting Nietzsche's "vitriolic attitude" towards Socrates in the *Twilight* chapter under discussion, Nehamas argues that the reason why Nietzsche so "despises" Socrates and the tradition he represents is the latter's dogmatism, whereas Nietzsche's genealogical approach to philosophy "reveals the very particular, very interested origins" from which our beliefs have emerged. *Pace* Nehamas, what I have sought to show in the course of this book is how Nietzsche's rhetorical practice is rife with dogmatic, and often blanket, statements.

and merely self-serving claims to spirituality" (Solomon, 204).[7] In a similar vein, Allison (2001, 84) notes that under the terms of Nietzsche's
genealogical method, the use of *ad hominem* to disclose the unconscious
drives informing "the higher-order constructions of literature, mythology,
religion, philosophy, politics, and the sciences" is deemed to be a very useful critical tool. "I'm not afraid to cite *names*," declares Nietzsche; "one
illustrates one's point of view very quickly when, here or there, one argues
ad hominem. For me, all this enhances clarity" (KSA 7: NF 1870–1871,
5[72]:109).

Clarity is indubitably what the so-called science of physiognomy and its
offshoot criminal anthropology sought to establish. An amalgam of phre-
nology and physiognomy, criminal anthropology rose to prominence
towards the end of the nineteenth century as a result of Cesare Lombroso's
1876 work, *Criminal Man*. In the first of its five editions (the last was
dated 1896–1897), the author details the results of his forensic study of
sixty-six 'criminal craniums' ('Criminal Craniums' is the title of the first
chapter of *Criminal Man*), sourced from mainly Italian museums and private collections. Noting the common atavistic features of his skull sample,
Lombroso infers that the closer the cranial resemblance is between an
individual and an ape, the closer that individual's behavior will be to its
hominoid ancestor. The first edition of *Criminal Man* closes with the
author's dual assertion that "criminals resemble savages and the colored
races" and that the facts presented in his book "clearly prove that the most
horrendous and inhuman crimes have a biological, atavistic origin in ani-
malistic instincts" (Lombroso 2007, 91). It is on the basis of this

---

[7] Solomon's (1996, 188–217) defense of *ad hominem* rests on the following arguments:
(1) When lawyers attack the testimony of an expert witness by questioning his or her moral
character, they are arguing *ad hominem*, but not fallaciously. (2) What justifies an *ad hominem* argument is the intrinsic connection between the thought and the thinker insofar as the
value of the former is in part dependent on the personal qualities of the latter. (3) "Nietzsche
presumes a substantial self which cannot be distinguished from its attributes, attitudes, and
ideas." And (4) Philosophical concepts do not exist in and of themselves "in some Platonic
heaven"; they are "culturally constructed and cultivated" and constitutive of the person who
lays claim to them.

particular type of biological determinism that Nietzsche speculates upon Socrates' mooted criminality.[8]

Nietzsche's speculation runs along the following syllogistic rails:

> *Premise 1*: Socrates is ugly.
> *Premise 2*: Ugliness is a physiological criminal trait (according to criminal anthropology).
> *Speculative conclusion*: "Was Socrates a typical criminal?" TI 'Socrates' 3, KSA 6:68)

Nietzsche's conclusion is so patently absurd—"absurdly rational," to misappropriate the oxymoron used by Nietzsche in the same segment—that one might be inclined to view it as an intentional parody of the syllogistic form. Support for such a reading can be found three segments later in Nietzsche's claim that syllogistic reasoning is itself a symptom of decadence:

> Is Socratic irony an expression of revolt? of rabble-*ressentiment* [*Pöbel-Ressentiment*]? As the member of an oppressed group, did Socrates take pleasure in the ferocity with which he could thrust his syllogistic knife? Did he avenge himself on the nobles he fascinated? … Is dialectics just a form of *revenge* for Socrates? ('Socrates' 7, KSA 6:70)

Note here the essentializing compound noun 'rabble-*ressentiment*' and its corresponding nouns 'revenge' and 'revolt'—a correspondence first established and concretized in *Daybreak* (see Chap. 3).[9] But if Nietzsche's rhetorical question regarding Socrates' posited criminality is little more than a harmless piece of rhetorical frivolity, are we to extend the same interpretive latitude to Nietzsche's sophistical distortion of Socrates' response to the physiognomist Zopyrus who told him that his features were those of a *"monstrum"*? ('Socrates' 3, KSA 6:69). As reported by Cicero in §80 of Book 4 of *Tusculan Disputations* (2002, 69), Socrates' frank rejoinder to Zopyrus was that vices were indeed innate in him (presumably in the sense

---

[8]Dahlkvist (2012, 142–143) believes that on the evidence available to us, the probability of Nietzsche not being familiar with Lombroso's theory is extremely slim: "Lombroso was a professor at the University of Turin when Nietzsche lived there, and was an immensely important figure in the contemporary scientific discourse on degeneration. And when for example the Swedish writer August Strindberg criticizes Nietzsche's understanding of the criminal in their correspondence, he does so by citing Lombroso to support his own outlook." Cited in Owen (2021, 56).

[9]Chapter 3 also contains an extended discussion on the essentializing effect of Nietzsche's compound nouns in BGE.

that vices are innate in us all), "but that he had cast them out by reason." Nietzsche construes this remark as an "admission" by Socrates of having anarchic instincts ('Socrates' 4, KSA 6:69), and then deploys this so-called admission as retrospective justification for linking the physiognomist's *monstrum* remark to criminal anthropology's pseudoscientific claim that "*monstrum in fronte, monstrum in animo*" [monster in the face, monster in the soul] ('Socrates' 3, KSA 6:69).

How seriously are we to take Nietzsche here? He asserts that "Socrates was the clown who made himself be taken *seriously*" ('Socrates' 5, KSA 6:70), but the same applies to Nietzsche's risible attempts to prove that Socrates was a decadent—attempts that appear to be as "bizarre" and "idiosyncratic" as, in Nietzsche's view, the Socratic equation "reason = virtue = happiness" (TI 'Socrates' 3–4, KSA 6:68–69). They appear somewhat less bizarre, however, when read in the context of Nietzsche's theory concerning the debilitating effects of ugliness. In a late *Twilight* chapter, he asserts that whereas beauty acts like a tonic, the sight of ugliness produces in us an involuntary visceral reaction: "Physiologically, everything ugly weakens and depresses people. It reminds them of decay, danger, deadly stupors; it actually drains them of strength. The effect of ugliness can be measured with a dynamometer." Nietzsche goes on to argue that as a result of this physiological reaction, "a *hatred* leaps up: What is it people hate when this happens? But there is no doubt: *the decline of their type*. They hate out of the deepest instinct of their species" (TI 'Skirmishes' 20, KSA 6:124). Note the dogmatism of Nietzsche's assertion that our visceral reaction to ugliness is rooted in the human species' instinctive hatred of human decay—the type of instinctive reaction, in fact, that a calm, patient, and non-judgmental critic would take pains to suppress. Equally dogmatic is Nietzsche's confident assertion that ugliness is "a sign and symptom of degeneration" (ibid.).

Once again, what this chapter has endeavored to show is the need for extreme vigilance on the part of the Nietzsche reader. Just as the title to Nietzsche's 1873 essay 'On Truth and Lies in a Nonmoral Sense' sends a mixed message to the reader insofar as the title's rhetorically provocative and morally loaded phrase 'truth and lies' belies the qualificatory 'nonmoral sense,' so *Twilight*'s subtitle 'How to Philosophize with a Hammer' leads the reader to expect BGE-grade aggression rather than the patience and magnanimity typical of *Twilight*. Similarly, just as the cumulative mode of argumentation in *Daybreak* serves to shore up Nietzsche's highly selective and tendentious genealogy of morals, so his philological bad faith in 'The Problem of Socrates' encourages the reader to acquiesce in his endorsement of a long-discredited pseudoscience, the leading proponent of which declared that criminals possess the atavistic traits of savages and that savages and the 'colored races' are one and the same.

REFERENCES

Allison, David B. 2001. *Reading the New Nietzsche: The Birth of Tragedy, The Gay Science, Thus Spoke Zarathustra, and On the Genealogy of Morals*. Lanham: Rowman & Littlefield.
Cicero. 2002. *Cicero on the Emotions: Tusculan Disputations 3 and 4*. Trans. Margaret Graver. Chicago: The University of Chicago Press.
Dahlkvist, Tobias. 2012. Nietzsche and medicine. In *Handbuch Nietzsche und die Wissenschaften*, ed. Helmut Heit and Lisa Heller, 138–154. Berlin: De Gruyter.
Dannhauser, Werner J. 1974. *Nietzsche's View of Socrates*. New York: Cornell University Press.
Lombroso, Cesare. 2007. *Criminal Man*. Trans. Mary Gibson and Nicole Hahn Rafter. Durham and London: Duke University Press.
Nehamas, Alexander. 1985. *Nietzsche: Life as Literature*. Cambridge: Harvard University Press.
Nietzsche, Friedrich. 2001a. *The Gay Science*. Trans. Josefine Nauckhoff. New York: Cambridge University Press.
———. 2001b. *Thus Spoke Zarathustra: A Book for All and None*. Trans. Adrian del Caro. New York: Cambridge University Press.
———. 2002. *Beyond Good and Evil: Prelude to a Philosophy of the Future*. Trans. Judith Norman. Cambridge: Cambridge University Press.
———. 2006a. *Daybreak: Thoughts on the Prejudices of Morality*. Trans. R. J. Hollingdale. Cambridge: Cambridge University Press.
———. 2006b. *The Anti-Christ, Ecce Homo, Twilight of the Idols*. Trans. Judith Norman. New York: Cambridge University Press.
Owen, David. 2021. Rhetorics of degeneration: Nietzsche, Lombroso, and Napoleon. *The Journal of Nietzsche Studies* 52 (1): 51–64.
Plato. 2005. *Euthyphhro, Apology, Crito, Phaedo, Phaedrus*. Trans. Harold North Fowler. Cambridge: Harvard University Press.
Solomon, Robert C. 1996. Nietzsche *ad hominem*: Perspectivism, personality and *ressentiment*. In *The Cambridge Companion to Nietzsche*, ed. Bernd Magnus and Kathleen M. Higgins, 180–222. Cambridge: Cambridge University Press.

CHAPTER 6

Conclusion

Abstract The book concludes with an inventory of Nietzsche's rhetorical figures—copious examples of which he would have encountered in his reading of Greek and Roman handbooks on rhetoric—and the following caveat. Notwithstanding Nietzsche's consummate oratorical skills and concomitant powers of persuasion, it would be a mistake to infer that all his work is a calculated, rhetorical performance. Militating against such an inference is the intensely personal, emotional, and visceral charge of his writing, together with the many prefatory confidences and confessions that he openly shares with his readers.

Keywords Nietzsche • Rhetorical devices • Classical rhetoric • Autobiography

My aim in this book has been to examine Nietzsche's rhetoric with a view to gauging its impact not only on his philosophical claims but on the critical faculties of his readers. The weight of this impact, I believe, is due in no small part to the panoply of rhetorical devices cataloged in the Greek and Roman handbooks on rhetoric and from which Nietzsche compiled his lecture notes on classical rhetoric while a professor at the University of Basel (Gilman et al. 1989, xi). One of the sources cited in these notes is the *Rhetorica ad Herennium* (circa 86–82 BCE), a seminal work of unknown origin but which in Nietzsche's day was still erroneously attributed to Cornificius. Book 4 of this treatise ([Cicero] 1904, 227–410) is a compendium of "the principles of embellishing style" deemed to be constitutive of oratory excellence. Among these principles is a list of ten rhetorical figures, or what the Ancients referred to as 'figures of diction,' namely, onomatopoeia, antonomasia, metonymy, periphrasis, hyperbaton, hyperbole, synecdoche, catachresis, metaphor, and allegory. A similar list appears in Nietzsche's aforesaid lecture notes (Rh. 53–55), but is expanded to include metalepsis, epithet, irony, anastrophe, and parenthesis. Each of these fifteen figures is stock in trade for Nietzsche. But in addition to these and of particular prominence in the preceding four case studies are the following stylistic embellishments, listed here in the numerical order in which they appear in the *Rhetorica*:

[XXI] paronomasia (wordplay)
[XXVIII] reduplication (the repetition of word(s) for the purpose of amplification)
[XXXIX] vivid description
[XLII] refining (either repeating or 'descanting' upon an idea)
[XLIII] dialogue (putting words into someone's mouth "in keeping with his character," but see my Chap. 5 critique of the words Nietzsche thrusts down Socrates' throat)
[XLVI] comparison, used for the purpose of embellishment, proof, clarification or vivification.

What the foregoing chapters have endeavored to show is how Nietzsche presses these embellishing arts into the service of argumentation. Nevertheless, notwithstanding Nietzsche's consummate oratorical skills and concomitant powers of persuasion, I am far from claiming that all his work is a calculated, rhetorical performance. On the contrary, I believe that any such claim is vulnerable to at least two objections. First, it is impossible to overlook the intensely personal, emotional, and visceral charge of Nietzsche's writing: by turns malicious and magnanimous, derisive and self-mocking, poignant and facetious, naked and masked, ropedancer and buffoon. A random sample might be, "Had we not welcomed the arts ... *Honesty* would lead to nausea and suicide" (GS 107, KSA 3:464), or "What? Does life also *require* the rabble? Are poisoned wells and stinking fires and soiled dreams and maggots required in life's bread?" (Z2 'On the Rabble,' KSA 4:124–127), or "To subtler nostrils, even this English Christianity bears the genuinely English odor of the very spleen and alcoholic dissipation against which it is rightly used as a remedy" (BGE 252, KSA 5:195–196), or "Every smallest step in the field of free thought, of a life shaped personally, has always had to be fought for with spiritual and bodily tortures" (D 18, KSA 3:31). Each of these statements is profoundly personal: The first is an autobiographical allusion to Nietzsche's implacable and self-depleting intellectual honesty; the second and third—bilious attacks on the rabble and the Englishman—would appear to emanate from "the very great stupidity" that lies deep within us all (BGE 231, KSA 5:170); while the martyrdom of the fourth is an elaboration of the honesty mentioned in the first.

A second objection to the hypothetical claim that Nietzsche is permanently in rhetorical mode is the non-rhetorical style of the confidences he shares with the reader, such as those in his late and quietly reflective prefaces to the two volumes of *Human*. In the first of these prefaces, he confesses to having sought shelter in either admiration or enmity, frivolity or stupidity. And when these could not be found, he admits to having needed "to enforce, falsify and invent a suitable fiction for myself … for my cure and self-restoration" (HH1 P1, KSA 2:14)—the same admission as the GS 107 "nausea and suicide" remark quoted above. In the second *Human* preface, he writes of his debilitating disgust at the "dreadful spectacle" of Wagner suddenly sinking down "helpless and shattered before the Christian cross" (an allusion to Wagner's *Parsifal*) and of the colossal disillusionment that ensued, "I was sick, more than sick" (HH2 P2, KSA 2:372). Similar confidences appear in the body of his texts, especially in *Zarathustra* where they are shared with the reader either through Zarathustra's dreams or through an assortment of allegorical figures, including Zarathustra's shadow or his eagle and serpent who in Part 3 of *Zarathustra* witness their master's breakdown and try to cajole him back to health (Z4 'The Convalescent,' KSA 4:270–277).

Above all, however, it is my contention that Nietzsche wrote in a style meticulously crafted to both captivate and capture his readers. And if, as he tells us in *Ecce Homo*, all his post-*Zarathustra* writings were intended to be "fish hooks" (EH 'BGE' 1, KSA 6:350), then we, as readers, need to exercise extreme caution in deciding when and when not to take the bait.

REFERENCES

[Cicero]. 1954. *Rhetorica ad Herennium*. Trans. Harry Caplan. Loeb Classical Library. Cambridge: Harvard University Press.

Gilman, Sander L., Carol Blair, and David J. Parent, eds. 1989. *Friedrich Nietzsche on Rhetoric and Language.* New York: Oxford University Press.

Nietzsche, Friedrich. 2001a. *The Gay Science.* Trans. Josefine Nauckhoff. New York: Cambridge University Press.

———. 2001b. *Thus Spoke Zarathustra: A Book for All and None.* Trans. Adrian del Caro. New York: Cambridge University Press.

———. 2002. *Beyond Good and Evil: Prelude to a Philosophy of the Future.* Trans. Judith Norman. Cambridge: Cambridge University Press.

———. 2006a. *Daybreak: Thoughts on the Prejudices of Morality.* Trans. R. J. Hollingdale. Cambridge: Cambridge University Press.

———. 2006b. *The Anti-Christ, Ecce Homo, Twilight of the Idols.* Trans. Judith Norman. New York: Cambridge University Press.

———. 2007. *Human, All Too Human: A Book for Free Spirits.* Trans. R. J. Hollingdale. Cambridge: Cambridge University Press.

APPENDIX

"The question of style" dominated Nietzsche scholarship from the late 1960s to the mid-1980s and is once again on the rise.[1] The question pertains to the relationship between thought and the mode(s) of expressing that thought, which in the case of Nietzsche largely translates into the question whether the aphoristic and/or figurative form of his work is intrinsic to its philosophical content or merely incidental. A brief review of what many interpreters have taken to be an intrinsic connection between Nietzsche's philosophy and his aphoristic style is provided in Chap. 1. Here in the Appendix, I shall provide an overview of those commentators who have interpreted Nietzsche's characteristic use of metaphor as an extension or elaboration of his theory of language.

The first scholars to engage directly with Nietzsche's figurative style of writing viewed as an organic outgrowth of his philosophical commitments were the French poststructuralists,[2] who took as their point of departure

[1] See, for example, Thomas (1999); Allison (2001); Del Caro (2004); second chapter of Babich (2006a, 19–36); Babich (2006b, 177–190); Strong (2013); and Lambek (2020).

[2] "The 'question of style' as a focal point in the interpretation of Nietzsche's text was first raised explicitly by Bernard Pautrat in *Versions du soleil* and it operates as well ... in Derrida's raising 'the question of writing' ('*c'est la question du style comme question de l'écriture*'); and in Lacoue-Labarthe's 'question of the text': 'Without [Nietzsche], the 'question' of the text would never have erupted, at least in the precise form that it has taken today.'" See Schrift (1996, 329). See also the first two essays in Lacoue-Labarthe (1993).

© The Author(s), under exclusive license to Springer Nature   107
Switzerland AG 2023
F. Cauchi, *Nietzsche's Rhetoric*,
https://doi.org/10.1007/978-3-031-42964-4

the Saussurean 'linguistic turn.' In his study of the structure of language, Saussure (2011, 66) held that "[t]he linguistic sign unites, not a thing and a name, but a concept and a sound-image. The latter is not the material sound, a purely physical thing, but the psychological imprint of the sound, the impression that it makes on our senses." Accordingly, if sound images ('signifiers') and their associated concepts ('signifieds') are not inherently connected to the world of objects they purport to represent, then the relation between sign and object is neither fixed nor universal—a conclusion reached by Nietzsche some forty years earlier. In his unfinished 1873 essay 'On Truth and Lies in a Nonmoral Sense,' Nietzsche asserts that far from articulating the essence of the thing named, language is merely a linguistic convention that reflects man's empirical relation to things. The words that we use to designate things, he writes, are irreducibly metaphorical. They are merely the last in a series of substitutive metaphors, each of which is "a suggestive transposition, a stammering translation" (TL 86, KSA 1:884), from one sphere to an entirely different sphere, i.e., from a nerve stimulus (sensation) to an image (perception) to a sound (word). It is this ineluctable metaphoricity of language which, to adopt two of Nietzsche's metaphors, unchains Western metaphysics from its sun of truth and authority (GS 125, KSA 3:480–482) and reduces the 'science' of logic, together with the grand conceptual systems of science and philosophy, to the skein of a spider's web (TL 85, KSA 1:882).[3]

Within the figurative economy of this reconceptualization of language, the trope is no longer seen as a handmaiden to thought, but as constitutive of language itself. Imbued with this knowledge, the newly "liberated intellect," writes Nietzsche in 'Truth and Lies,' smashes to pieces the traditional linguistic binaries of literal and figurative, truth and untruth, and with the resulting rubble of metaphors plays ironically, intuitively, and audaciously (TL 90, KSA 1:888). It is this notion of play that informs Jacques Derrida's reconfiguration of hermeneutics as the interpretation of an interpretation rather than a retrieval of meaning. In his 1966 lecture 'Structure, Sign, and Play,' Derrida (2001, 353–354) cites Nietzsche's critique of metaphysics and, in particular, his substitution of "play, interpretation, and sign (sign without present truth)" for the concepts of Being and truth, as a major catalyst in exposing the fiction of a center or fixed origin around which our systems of thought and language have

---

[3] I concur with Strong (2013, 511–12) that Nietzsche's early work on rhetoric "informs all his work."

traditionally been structured.[4] Once this 'lie' (see 'Truth and Lies') has been exposed—i.e., the lie of essence, substance, origin, and transcendence, or what Derrida variously refers to as 'the metaphysics of presence,' 'the law of central presence,' or the 'transcendental signified'—the structure's organizing principle implodes, opening the way to a play of meaning.[5] Taking these ideas forward and applying them directly to Nietzsche's work were Bernard Pautrat and Sarah Kofman, both of whom interpret Nietzsche's texts along the Derridean lines glossed here by Goldschmit (2011, 381): "To think the metaphor 'as such,' that is to say, to think there is no metaphor as such, to think it by metaphorizing it is to think the unity of metaphoricity and non-metaphoricity as the essence of language, to think the erasure of the present in language, in other words to think the trace or writing."

Pautrat (1971, 10) wrote the first draft of his monograph on Nietzsche while still a student at the École normale supérieure, where, in the winter of 1969–70, Derrida held a seminar on the status of metaphor within philosophical discourse. In the preface to his monograph, Pautrat (1971, 9) outlines the two axes along which his analysis will proceed: A theoretical axis relating to the metaphoricity of language and an interpretive axis relating to the metaphorical power of language in Nietzsche's work. The title of Pautrat's book, *Versions du soleil*, pertains to the heliological systems of Zoroaster, Plato, Hegel, and Nietzsche. To summarize: In the Zoroastrian myth of solar fire, which Hegel uses to illustrate belief in a mystical identity between form and content, the sun is neither symbol nor metaphor but the immediacy of the divine, the Absolute. In Plato's solar system, the sun symbolizes the Idea, or what Nietzsche in *Twilight of the Idols* refers to—and ridicules—as the "true world" (see TI 'How the "True

---

[4] The other two catalysts cited by Derrida (2001) are Freud and Heidegger.

[5] "Henceforth, it was necessary to begin thinking that there was no center, that the center could not be thought in the form of a present-being, that the center had no natural site, that it was not a fixed locus but a function, a sort of nonlocus in which an infinite number of sign-substitutions came into play" (Derrida 2001, 353). I am grateful to Trevor Hope for pointing out that Derrida's notion of play ('*jeu*'), usually translated as 'freeplay,' has been misunderstood as referring to a radically undetermined view of language and meaning. In 'Structure, Sign, and Play,' argues Hope, 'free' play does not mean an anarchic rejection of all ideas of system, but is intended to capture the sense of movement within a system—a kind of looseness or, to put it more abstractly, freedom from the rigid determination associated with center and origin. In other words, the sign-substitutions are infinite in the sense that linguistic value can never be fully determined because we can never exhaust all the possible relations between signifier and signified.

World" Finally Became a Fable: The History of an Error,' KSA 6:80–81). In Hegel's heliology, the sun is Absolute Knowledge, reached through a dialectical movement of self-knowledge. And in Nietzsche's heliology, the figurative "great noon" of *Zarathustra* is interpreted by Pautrat as an awakening, the same awakening that in the *Twilight* chapter cited above is depicted as the dawning of a new day. This new day, contends Pautrat (1971, 26–27), goes beyond Plato's metaphysics of truth and Hegel's dialectical movement of negation because within Nietzsche's heliological system the new day is always succeeded by another new day. Just as the setting sun marks the descent, *Untergang*, and death—i.e., negation—of one day, it necessarily ushers in the dawn of the next: "in Nietzsche, circularity makes it possible to think ... self-transcendence as reversal per se."

What I find most arresting in Pautrat's reading of the four heliologies is its conceptual linking of Hegel's dialectical movement of negation with Zarathustra's concept of *Untergang*—a correlation that implicitly challenges Deleuze's (1983, 8) once influential, but now discredited, claim that Nietzsche's work is fundamentally anti-Hegelian.[6] Contra Deleuze, Pautrat (1971, 20) asserts that the proximity between Hegel and Nietzsche is undeniable, once one recognizes how insistent the work of the negative is in Nietzsche's metaphors of the circle, the ring, the serpent, and the wheel. I draw the same conclusion (Cauchi 2022, 101–136) in my comparative reading of Hegel's 'labor of the negative' and the negation entailed in Zarathustra's doctrine of self-overcoming. But whereas Pautrat grounds his interpretation in Nietzsche's tropic circles and derives therefrom an affirmative reading of Nietzsche, I ground mine in Zarathustra's surgical metaphor of spirit cutting into life (see Z2 'On the Famous Wise Men,' KSA 4:134). On my reading, Nietzsche's act of self-transcendence—poignantly narrated in *Zarathustra*—entails copious bloodshed, a long convalescence, and the type of spectral etiolation figured in Zarathustra's shadow (see Z4 'The Shadow,' KSA 4:339–341, cited in Chap. 3).

Written in the same year as Pautrat's *Versions de soleil*, Kofman's *Nietzsche et la métaphore* (1971)[7] traces Nietzsche's "strategic" use of metaphor in his three early works: *The Birth of Tragedy, Philosophy in the Tragic Age of the Greeks*, and 'Truth and Lies.' Kofman begins her survey with *Birth*, a work in which Nietzsche reads the Greek gods Apollo and Dionysus as

---

[6] See Breazeale (1975, 158–161); Houlgate (1986, 7); and Jurist (2000, 27).
[7] *Nietzsche et la métaphore* first appeared as an article in the French journal *Poetique* (Kofman 1971).

figurative representations of the agon between appearance and reality, form and chaos, measure and ecstasy, respectively. Kofman reminds us of Nietzsche's own reflection on *Birth*, namely that he should have sung like a poet, rather than talked like a scholar (AS 3, KSA 1:15). Had he done so, however, the end product would doubtless have been only marginally less objectionable to his professorial peers than the essay he did pen with flagrant disregard for the academic conventions of philosophic discourse.[8] Moving onto the posthumously published *Philosophy in the Tragic Age of the Greeks*, Kofman (1993, 13–14) cites a passage in which Nietzsche compares the philosopher to the Greek dramatist. Just as the latter can only stammer the "alien tongue" of intuition that music utters directly, so the former has to resort to the language of scientific reflection to impart his "philosophical intuition." The resulting philosophical discourse, continues Nietzsche, is "basically a metaphorical and entirely unfaithful translation [of intuition] into a totally different sphere and speech" (PTAG 3; KSA 1:187). Turning to Nietzsche's unfinished 1873 essay 'Truth and Lies,' Kofman (1993, 60–73) compares Nietzsche's intuitive man, who "speaks only in forbidden metaphors and in unheard-of combinations" (TL 90, KSA 1: 889), to Nietzsche's use of metaphors in 'Truth and Lies'—i.e., beehive, tower, pyramid, columbarium, and spider—by means of which he ridicules the scientist's complex conceptual systems. I make the same observation in Chap. 2.

These early works, asserts Kofman (1993, 17–18), "introduce new relations between philosophy, art, and science." Whereas previously, philosophy and science had "repressed" the use of images or similes in a bid to be more convincing, Nietzsche "inaugurates a type of philosophy which deliberately uses metaphors" to unmask the metaphorical status of concepts in language and science. This strategy, continues Kofman, is not just

---

[8] In a 1979 essay entitled 'The Fable (Literature and Philosophy),' Lacoue-Labarthe (1993, 10) argues that *The Birth of Tragedy* was not entirely and not unequivocally a "youthful" text. Indeed, although Lacoue-Labarthe does not spell this out for us, it is intimated in Nietzsche's self-critique of the book as one in which "my youthful courage and suspicion vented itself—what an *impossible* book was bound to grow out of a task so at odds with youth! ... a youthful work ... independent, standing defiantly on its own two feet even where it appears to bow before an authority and its own veneration" (AS 2, KSA 1:13). Lacoue-Labarthe (1993, 10) astutely discerns in the work "at least two languages: one in which the greater part of post-Hegelian metaphysics and of metaphysics plain and simple is confirmed; and another (but quite often it is the same one in the process of coming undone) in which 'deconstruction' is already under way."

a playing with metaphors, but play "of a 'formidable seriousness,' for it is designed ... to obliterate precisely the opposition between play and seriousness, dream and reality, [and] to show that 'mathematical expression is not a part of the essence of philosophy' [KSA 7: NF 1872–1873, 19[62]:439]."

Playing with metaphors is a remarkably apt description of Derrida's hermeneutic method in *Éperons: Les Styles de Nietzsche* [*Spurs: Nietzsche's Styles*]. Emulating—one might almost say outdoing—the intuitive man of Nietzsche's 'Truth and Lies,' Derrida (1979, 37–41) speaks mostly in metaphors and unheard-of combinations in a metonymical game of word association. The titular spurs is the operative case in point. In Derrida's hands, the word 'spur' is deployed as a metaphor for style, which then metamorphoses into "a quill or a stylus ... a stiletto, or even a rapier." The rapier spurs Derrida on to spur's half rhyme 'spar,' in the act of which the stylistic spur "perforates even as it parries," warding off "the terrifying, blinding, mortal threat [of that] which *presents* itself, which obstinately thrusts itself into view" (Derrida is as dramatic as he is ludic). And in the thrust and parry of the "style-spur, the spurring style," Derrida fancifully imagines the furling and unfurling of Nietzsche's forgotten umbrella. Lastly, Derrida notes that the German noun 'spur' means "trace, track, wake, sign, mark," which tacitly recuperates the image of the quill or the stylus as metonyms for writing—hence, style. In short, Derrida's reading of Nietzsche's styles, as he freely admits at the end of *Spurs*, is "open, cryptic, and parodying." Simultaneously "open and closed, or each in turn, folded/unfolded, it is just an umbrella that you couldn't use. You might just as soon forget it."

In contrast to Derrida's extra-textual wordplay, Gilles Deleuze focuses on Nietzsche's inter- and intratextual figures of play. In his widely influential *Nietzsche et la philosophie* (1963)—the same monograph in which he construes Nietzsche's corpus as fundamentally anti-Hegelian—Deleuze takes four symbols from Nietzsche's *Zarathustra* (1883–1884) and conflates them with the figure of Dionysus in *Birth* (1872) and *Ecce Homo* (1888). These symbols are the game of dice and the figurative triad chaos—fire—constellation, which Deleuze (1983, 29–30) systematically interprets with breathtaking speed and assurance. He begins with the game of dice, the constitutive parts of which he construes as follows: The shaking of the dice symbolizes 'chaos'; the throwing of the dice symbolizes the affirmation of 'chance'; the constellation or configuration of the thrown dice symbolizes the affirmation of 'necessity'; and the game of dice per se emblematizes 'will to power,' "for only the will to power is capable of affirming all chance." Fire is said to be "the element of transformations which has no opposite"; it is thus non-dialectical. And the figurative triad is said to bring together "all the elements of the myth of Dionysus. Or rather these images form the truly Dionysian game. The *playthings* of the child Dionysus; multiple affirmation … unity being affirmed of multiplicity; the constellation borne by Dionysus, Ariadne in the sky like a dancing star."

As Pecora (1986, 42) points out, however, Deleuze's serial assertions (1983, 188–189)—that "Becoming is being, multiplicity is unity, chance is necessity"; that affirmation is "the enjoyment and play of its own difference"; and that this play of difference is in direct opposition to Hegel's dialectical labor of the negative[9]—entirely overlook the struggle, opposition, and suffering palpably present in Nietzsche's thought.[10] I agree. But if we set aside Deleuze's rhetorical excess and overplaying of untrammeled play, his intertextual linking of Nietzsche's tropes elucidates a plausible continuity of ideas between the affirmative character of Dionysus in *Birth* and the affirmation of the being of becoming in *Zarathustra*.[11]

Fast forwarding to the twenty-first century, Allison (2001, 74–78) reads Nietzsche's '*figurative*' use of language—Allison's italics, here, a timely reminder that for Nietzsche language is constitutively figurative—as the most effective way of conveying the dynamic flux of the world, or what Nietzsche refers to as 'will to power.'[12] Echoing the French poststructuralists, Allison interprets Nietzsche's decision to cast his thought in rhetorical forms of language—those forms which the Western

[9] For an extended discussion on the parallels between Hegel and Nietzsche's labor of the negative, see Cauchi (2022, 101–136).

[10] "Deleuze's unfortunate—and perhaps wishful—*idealization* of Nietzsche's work," writes Pecora (1986, 47), "amount[s] to a very interesting revision of Nietzsche's writings that systematically purges them of the 'human-all-too-human' marks of their own inception, marks Nietzsche is always very careful to leave visible—desire, especially desire for 'the truth'; struggle, against one's own heritage, against one's 'instincts'; suffering; opposition; tension; reflection; and, perhaps in the end, the inevitable error of reflection at the very heart of one's need for it."

[11] Deleuze (1983, 12–14) holds that Nietzsche's resurrection in his last works of the Dionysus of his first work is due to Nietzsche's recognition of the two "essential innovations" in *Birth*, namely life affirmation and the fundamental opposition between Dionysus and Socrates. These insights, continues Deleuze, had been overshadowed in *Birth* by the combined influences of Hegel, Schopenhauer, and Wagner.

[12] Many scholars appear to overlook the figurative status of Nietzsche's concept of 'will to power.'

philosophical tradition permanently exiled to the 'impure' realm of literary invention—as an implicit rejection of that tradition. By embracing the "essentially unstable" rhetorical figures of aphorism, apothegm, image, simile, and metaphor, submits Allison, Nietzsche repudiates philosophy's delimiting conventions of strict definition, rigorous logical argument, and the principle of identity (*A* is *A*). What is noteworthy here is Allison's inclusion of the aphorism in his list of fundamentally unstable forms of expression. The aphorism, he contends, is "essentially *metaphorical.*" Resisting "formalism and catechism," it is "open-ended," requiring for its completion and intelligibility an interpretive operation on the part of the reader (cf. GM Pref. 8, KSA 5:255). That operation, he continues, "induces the reader to gather resemblances, to cull differences, to collect similarities, to compare and contrast markedly different cases, and to assemble all these, however briefly, and to thereby exhibit, to make manifest, the very movement of thought. In this sense, the metaphor is an instrument *for* thinking and not an end-point or terminus of thought."

Pace Allison, my overarching objective in these four case studies has been to detail the extent to which many of Nietzsche's aphorisms are emphatically not open-ended. As I have endeavored to show, rather than offering themselves as an instrument for thinking, they oftentimes shut down thought altogether.

References

Allison, David B. 2001. *Reading the New Nietzsche: The Birth of Tragedy, The Gay Science, Thus Spoke Zarathustra, and On the Genealogy of Morals.* Lanham: Rowman & Littlefield.

Babich, Babette E. 2006a. *Words in Blood, Like Flowers: Philosophy and Poetry, Music and Eros in Hölderlin, Nietzsche, and Heidegger.* Albany: SUNY Press.

———. 2006b. The *Genealogy of Morals* and right reading: On the Nietzschean aphorism and the art of the polemic. In *Nietzsche's 'On the Genealogy of Morals': Critical Essays*, ed. Christa Davis Acampora, 177–190. Lanham: Rowman & Littlefield.

Breazeale, Daniel. 1975. The Hegel-Nietzsche problem. *Nietzsche-Studien* 4: 146–164.

Cauchi, Francesca. 2022. *Zarathustra's Moral Tyranny: Spectres of Kant, Hegel and Feuerbach.* Edinburgh: Edinburgh University Press.

Cicero. 2002. *Cicero on the Emotions: Tusculan Disputations 3 and 4.* Trans. Margaret Graver. Chicago: The University of Chicago Press.

Del Caro, Adrian. 2004. Nietzsche's rhetoric on the grounds of philology and hermeneutics. *Philosophy & Rhetoric* 37 (2): 101–122.

Deleuze, Gilles. 1983. *Nietzsche and Philosophy*. Trans. Hugh Tomlinson. New York: Columbia University Press. Original edition: 1962. *Nietzsche et la philosophie*. Paris: Presses universitaires de France.

Derrida, Jacques. 1979. *Éperons: Les Styles de Nietzsche/Spurs: Nietzsche's Styles*. Trans. Barbara Harlow. Chicago: University of Chicago Press.

———. 2001. *Writing and Difference*. Trans. Alan Bass. London: Routledge.

Goldschmit, Marc. 2011. Le movement métaphorique de l'histoire sous la peau métaphysique du langage: Notes sur un cours inédit de Jacques Derrida (novembre 1964-mars 1965). *Revue de Métaphysique et de Morale* 71 (3): 371–384.

Houlgate, Stephen. 1986. *Hegel, Nietzsche and the Criticism of Metaphysics*. Cambridge: Cambridge University Press.

Jurist, Elliot L. 2000. *Beyond Hegel and Nietzsche: Philosophy, Culture, and Agency*. Cambridge: The MIT Press.

Kofman, Sarah. 1971. Nietzsche et la métaphore. *Poétique* 5: 77–98.

———. 1993. *Nietzsche and Metaphor*. Trans. Duncan Large. London: The Athlone Press. Original edition: 1972. *Nietzsche et la métaphore*. Paris: Payot.

Lacoue-Labarthe, Phillipe. 1993. *The Subject of Philosophy*, ed. Thomas Trezise. Trans. T. Trezise, H. J. Silverman et al. Minneapolis: University of Minnesota Press.

Lambek, Simon. 2020. Nietzsche's rhetoric: Dissonance and reception. *Epoché* 25 (1): 57–80.

Nietzsche, Friedrich. 1992. *Philosophy and Truth: Selections from Nietzsche's Notebooks of the Early 1870's*. Trans. Daniel Breazeale. Atlantic Highlands: Humanities Press.

———. 2001a. *The Gay Science*. Trans. Josefine Nauckhoff. New York: Cambridge University Press.

———. 2001b. *Thus Spoke Zarathustra: A Book for All and None*. Trans. Adrian del Caro. New York: Cambridge University Press.

———. 2006. *The Anti-Christ, Ecce Homo, Twilight of the Idols, and Other Writings*. Trans. Judith Norman. New York: Cambridge University Press.

———. 2007a. *The Birth of Tragedy and Other Writings*. Trans. Ronald Speirs. New York: Cambridge University Press.

———. 2007b. *On the Genealogy of Morality*. Trans. Carol Diethe. New York: Cambridge University Press.

Pautrat, Bernard. 1971. *Versions du soleil: figures et système de Nietzsche*. Paris: Éditions du Seuils.

Pecora, Vincent P. 1986. Deleuze's Nietzsche and post-structuralist thought. *Substance* 14 (3): 34–50.

Saussure, Ferdinand de. 2011. *Course in General Linguistics.* Trans. Wade Baskin. New York: Columbia University Press.

Schrift, Alan D. 1996. Nietzsche's French legacy. In *The Cambridge Companion to Nietzsche*, ed. Bernd Magnus and Kathleen M. Higgins, 323–355. New York: Cambridge University Press.

Strong, Tracy B. 2013. In defense of rhetoric: Or how hard it is to take a writer seriously: The case of Nietzsche. *Political Theory* 41 (4): 507–555.

Thomas, Douglas. 1999. *Reading Nietzsche Rhetorically.* New York and London: The Guildford Press.

INDEX[1]

---

[1] Note: Page numbers followed by 'n' refer to notes.

Heidegger, M., 109n4
Hill, Kevin R., 14n1
Hillis Miller, J., 16n5
Hinman, L. M., 83n20
Homonymy, 17n6, 19, 20, 23, 24,
 29, 78–80
Houlgate, S., 110n6
Hume, D., 60n2, 68
Hyperbole, 9, 10, 17, 18, 18n8, 27,
 34, 34n1, 39, 104

I
Ignoble, 10, 28, 29, 57–59, 63,
 64, 76, 80
Instinct, 28, 30, 59, 68–74,
 69n10, 76, 80, 83, 89,
 91, 92, 94, 96, 97, 99,
 101, 113n10

J
Janaway, C., 47n16
Judgments, affective-evaluative, 60
Jurist, E. L., 110n6

K
Kant, I., 2, 3, 9, 14, 14n1,
 14n2, 15, 20n9, 22,
 34, 89
 Critique of Pure Reason, 14
 'thing in itself,' *see Ding an sich*,
 14, 30, 62, 73, 83,
 83n20, 88
 transcendental idealism, 14, 18
Kaufmann, W., 7
Kofman, S., 7, 8, 17n7,
 109–111, 110n7
Kopp, D., 14n2, 15n3

L
Lacoue-Labarthe, P., 14n1, 20n10,
 107n2, 111n8
Lamarckism, 78n17
Lampert, L., 38n8
Lange, F., 14n2
Language
 Nietzsche's theory of, 5, 6, 6n4
 Saussure's theory of, 108
Leiter, B., 59, 60
Lineage, 74, 77, 78
 See also Breeding
Lombroso, C., 99, 100n8
 See also Anthropology, criminal;
 Determinism, biological;
 Physiognomy
Lupo, L., 69n10

M
Magnanimity, 11, 88–102
Magnus, B., 5n3
Malice, 11, 47, 53, 88–102
Man, Paul de., 5
Martyrs, 43–48
May, S., 37n7, 49n17, 72n13
Metaphor, 6, 16n5, 17, 25, 26,
 29, 68n9, 83, 89, 104,
 107–112, 114
Migotti, M., 64n7
Mitchell, J., 60, 61
Morality
 'master morality', 72 (*see also* Noble;
 Pathos of distance)
 as obedience to custom, 4, 10,
 27, 36–43
 'slave morality,' 50, 72, 72n12, 74
 (*see also* Ressentiment; Revenge)
Morals, genealogy of, 9, 34, 42, 101
 See also Genealogy

Printed in the USA
CPSIA information can be obtained
at www.ICGtesting.com
LVHW010854241123
764805LV00006B/87

9 783031 429637